Cyril Clark, Lang, — Gladie — Webster, Leslie Clark
Bentinck

PHNOM - PENH
CAMBODIA

LE ROYAL

HOTEL

D1605506

RAFFLES HOTEL, SINGAPORE.

GRAND HOTEL D'ANGKOR

H. VERGOZ

CAMBODGE

ASIA'S
LEGENDARY HOTELS

THE ROMANCE OF TRAVEL

WILLIAM WARREN

PHOTOGRAPHY BY JILL GOCHER

PERIPLUS EDITIONS
Singapore • Hong Kong • Indonesia

Published by Periplus Editions (HK) Ltd, with editorial
offices at 130 Joo Seng Road, #06-01 Singapore
368357.

Copyright © 2007 Periplus Editions (HK) Ltd
Photographs © 2007 Jill Gocher

ISBN 13 978 0 7946 0174 4
ISBN 10 0 7946 0174 X

Distributed by:

Asia Pacific
Berkeley Books Pte Ltd, 130 Joo Seng Road
#06-01, Singapore 368357.
Tel: (65) 6280 1330; Fax: (65) 6280 6290
E-mail: inquiries@periplus.com.sg
www.periplus.com

North America, Latin America and Europe
Tuttle Publishing, 364 Innovation Drive,
North Clarendon, Vermont 05759, USA.
Tel: 1 (802) 773 8930; Fax: 1 (802) 773 6993
E-mail: info@tuttlepublishing.com
www.tuttlepublishing.com

Japan
Tuttle Publishing, Yaekari Building, 3F, 5-4-12 Osaki,
Shinagawa-ku, Tokyo 141-0032.
Tel: (81) 3 5437 0171; Fax: (81) 3 5437 0755
E-mail: tuttle-sales@gol.com

First edition
11 10 09 08 07
5 4 3 2 1

Printed in Singapore

Page 1: Most of Asia's legendary hotels, especially
those in the tropics, were built in the days before
air-conditioning, when high ceilings and open
verandahs were essential for catching any passing
breeze. Here a plantation chair and a handy table
for afternoon drinks provide a view of the luxuriant
garden at the Amangalla.

Page 2: A staircase with wrought-iron railings leads
to upper floors in the lobby of the Taj Mahal Palace
and Tower. Molded stucco decorations at the top of
archways and columns and in the ceiling were often
features of such neo-classical structures.

Right: Evening view across Lake Pichola from the
Shiv Niwas Palace toward the Lake Palace Hotel in
Udaipur. Both are former royal residences which
have been converted into hotels, a trend that has
become increasingly popular in India's Rajasthan
region where princely states remained semi-inde-
pendent during British rule.

Page 6: Comfortable wicker furniture provides
numerous spots for conversation over tea or cooling
drinks in the spacious public spaces of the Raffles
Hotel. The white columns and marble floors offer a
contrast to the tropical foliage just outside.

CONTENTS

the
ROMANCE
of TRAVEL

I stayed in my first historic Asian hotel on my first visit to the region in the late 1950s. It was Frank Lloyd Wright's famous Imperial Hotel in Tokyo and I still remember the sense of severe disillusionment I felt when I entered the lobby late on a summer afternoon after an endless flight across the Pacific aboard one of Pan American's China Clippers.

Exactly what I was expecting I can't say; probably something that would immediately confirm that I was in Japan rather than Los Angeles or Honolulu. What I found instead was a low, oddly uninviting structure, built of reddish lava stone, suggesting the dark claustrophobia of a Mayan temple rather than the light, airy quality I perceived as distinctively Japanese. It certainly had an interesting history as one of the very few buildings in Tokyo to survive the catastrophic earthquake of 1923 and the fire bombing of World War II.

As I wandered through its long, dimly-lit corridors and tried to shave with the use of a mirror set about four feet from the bathroom floor, I summoned up little sense of the romance of staying in one of the world's most legendary hotels. Perhaps other guests were similarly affected or the owners simply decided it was too "old-fashioned" for the modern image Tokyo was bent on swiftly acquiring.

In any event, the old Imperial disappeared a year or so later, with only a few voices raised in protest and was replaced by an ultra-modern creation where you really could be just about anywhere on Earth.

This was happening in other places too, as I discovered on subsequent travels. The great mass tourist boom was then just getting underway in Asia and as it gathered momentum whole cities were being transformed, not just their physical appearance but also in some cases their very personalities. Soon it was getting harder and harder to tell where you were from a superficial view and even more if you were staying in one of the countless hotels that had materialized along with everything else.

But my own perceptions and priorities were changing as well. Increasingly, I found myself trying to discover ways to get behind these bland contemporary façades that concealed the real cities; and as often as not the solution proved to be no more difficult than finding and booking a room in a hotel rich in local history. I was surprised at the number that were still in business, some precariously clinging to life amid all the unimaginative new construction, others lovingly restored by owners sensitive to their importance; and for me, they proved to be rare havens where the distinctive flavor of the past could be recaptured. On later visits to Tokyo, I even felt a powerful nostalgia about Wright's Imperial and wished that some way could have been found to preserve its gloomy glory, which in retrospect, didn't seem so anachronistic after all.

During a certain period, almost every major Asian city had at least one hotel that seemed to encapsulate its essence to visitors from afar and sometimes they had several. The names of these places spread through old travel guides, through the colorful luggage stickers that adorned steamer trunks, sometimes simply by word of mouth, from one knowledgeable traveler to another.

I am talking here, of course, about another, long-ago age of travel, when people went mostly by ship or train and took their time about it, staying for weeks or months in one place along the way. Arriving at such exotic destinations as Bombay (known today, alas, as Mumbai), Rangoon (Yangon), Singapore or Bangkok, they wanted comfort, even luxury, a home away from home. Uniformed representatives

Page 8: To Somerset Maugham, Singapore's Raffles Hotel stood for "all the fables of the exotic east." Starting as a simple bungalow on Beach Road in 1887, it grew into one of the most famous hotels in Asia, as shown in this picture taken in the 1930s when it was a gathering place for locals and international travelers.
Left: The buildings that make up the Amangalla date back several hundred years. The hotel is situated within the walls of Galle Fort, recently declared a UNESCO World Heritage Site.
Top: The extensively renovated interior of the Amangalla once played host to Dutch and British soldiers.

met them on arrival and conveyed them and their often copious luggage to the hotel in question, which was nearly always only a short distance away from the port or railway station.

Nearly all of these establishments were built toward the end of the 19th century, or in the early 20th, and most reflected pseudo-classical styles that had emerged in British India. They had vast lobbies (in which the newcomer was more than likely to run into a wandering friend or two), restaurants that served familiar food along with a few more exotic native dishes, enormous rooms usually divided

into several separate areas for living and sleeping, long corridors and impressively large staffs (in 1912, the Raffles Hotel was said to have 250 staff) ready to attend to one's every need. If the climate was tropical, as it often was, there were broad verandahs on which to relax in the early morning or late afternoon, ample ventilation to catch any passing breeze, mosquito netting over the beds and sometimes bathing facilities that consisted of huge jars from which one splashed cool water with the aid of a dipper (always worth an amusing mention in letters back home). In more temperate places, like the hill stations that were such a popular feature of colonial life, there were lap rugs, blankets, hot-water bottles and fireplaces regularly kept stoked on chilly evenings.

Later, in a number of prosperous ports of call such as Hong Kong, some hotels rose to such dizzying heights as eight or nine stories and offered such innovations as lifts; but the majority of them were relatively low buildings that sprawled over extensive landscaped gardens, with plenty of room for a stroll away from the teeming city streets outside.

An Englishwoman named Alice Beaumont was somewhat unusual in that she set out alone on a grand tour of Southeast Asia in 1902, but her reactions to where she stayed were typical of other travelers. Disembarking at the wharf in Rangoon, she duly noted in her diary: "I climb into the cab of an elderly Hindoo [sic] gentleman who spirits me away from the dock... Our destination is the new Strand Hotel, opened only last year by the estimable Sarkies Brothers... From the chalk white façade to the 'chess-board' tiles that embellish the lobby, everything about

Top: When a ballroom was added in 1920, the Raffles Hotel became a permanent fixture on Singapore's burgeoning social scene. Ballroom dances were regularly held until the outbreak of World War II.
Right: The Raffles Hotel began life as a simple 10-room bungalow before two new wings were constructed in 1890, marking it out as one of the leading hotels in the region.

the Strand evokes the sort of luxury that has been sorely missed on my long journey from England." The Raffles Hotel offered a similar refuge in Singapore ("I occupy the mornings touring this ever-alluring metropolis, the afternoons writing in the shade of the Palm Court before retiring to the Tiffin Room around tea time to plot my next step in this long trek"), as did the Oriental in Bangkok ("My room is supremely comfortable, with huge shutters opening out on to a tropical garden") and the Metropole in Hanoi ("suitably grand for a city newly honored as Indochina's capital").

It might be noted that Miss Beaumont actually met her future husband during one of those plotting sessions at Raffles' Tiffin Room and became engaged to him while exploring Angkor in Cambodia three months later. Excerpts from her diaries were published in 2000, together with an account of a parallel journey made by her great nephew, who stayed in many of the same hotels.

Despite their physical similarities, each great hotel had a distinctive ambiance all its own or acquired one over the years. Taking tea in the grand, gilded lobby of Hong Kong's Peninsula, for example, you had a panoramic view of Chinese junks plying the busy harbor and white buildings climbing dramatically up the Peak on the other side. The Raffles had the private Palm Court that so appealed to Miss Beaumont on hot afternoons, a billiard table under which a tiger was supposedly discovered and a Long Bar where the potent Singapore Sling was first concocted. The splendid Taj Mahal in Bombay overlooked the Gateway of India, the first thing countless arriving Englishmen and their memsahibs saw of the subcontinent and offered special rooms for the personal servants who often accompanied guests. From the art deco lobby of the Cathay, where sleek Chinese ladies showed off their shimmering silk gowns, one could ascend by lift to a roof garden overlooking the Bund, that highly visible concentration of Shanghai's power and wealth.

All kinds of travelers turned up in such settings—royalty, both genuine and bogus; dignitaries representing some government or other and suave conmen looking for a score; globe-trotting stars or stage and screen and world-weary socialites;

Left: The Ananda Spa is spread over 21,000 square feet (1,950 square meters) and offers dozens of treatments incorporating Ayurvedic and Western techniques. The heated outdoor lap pool offers breathtaking views of the Himalayas.
Top: The Taj Lake Palace in Udaipur was conceived as a private retreat and is accessible only by boat. It is perhaps best remembered as one of the magnificent locations used in the James Bond film Octopussy.

writers in search of fresh material to fire their imagination and usually finding it; even a few of what would soon be known as ordinary tourists, though well-heeled ones on the whole.

Some left lasting impressions: Somerset Maugham, for instance, seems to have stayed at just about every historic hotel in Asia and a remarkable number have commemorated that fact by naming a suite after him. Noel Coward was almost as ubiquitous, adding to his (and the hotel's) renown by writing *Private Lives* in just four days while confined by the flu to a suite at the Cathay. For five years, until the Japanese rudely interrupted his comfortable life, General Douglas MacArthur made his home in a penthouse atop the Manila Hotel, where it is still proudly preserved.

World War II marked the end of this era of leisurely travel, abetted by a dozen other more local conflicts that followed in its wake. One by one, willingly or otherwise, the colonials departed, carrying their memories and souvenirs off to homelands some of them only dimly remembered; new rulers took their place, with a different set of aspirations; new city centers rose, often out of near-total ruins and often, too, far from the old ones; air travel became the preferred mode of transport, though curiously, despite the greater speed that resulted, there appeared to be less time to experience places than there had been before.

The old hotels faced a growing dilemma. They had been built for a breed of traveler who seemed suddenly to have vanished, not for group tours who barely slept in their rooms or businessmen who wanted instant communication with foreign countries and all sorts of other novelties. Economic considerations were even more serious. Many of the rambling structures were in deplorable condition, suffering either from effects of war or too many years of neglect and frequently changing management. Roofs leaked, floorboards creaked, rising damp discolored the walls. Money was needed to bring them back to their former splendor, and a lot of it. Still more was needed for the large staffs still required to tend those generously proportioned suites and public rooms, not to mention for the modern bathroom fixtures and air-conditioning systems everybody now

Top: The four Sarkies brothers, Armenians who founded several of Asia's most famous hotels in the late 19th century, among them the Eastern & Oriental in Penang, Raffles in Singapore, and the Strand in Yangon (Rangoon).
Right: The lobby of the Raffles Hotel, each floor containing lounges for guests. The venerable hotel was extensively renovated at the end of the 1980s and is now preserved as a national heritage structure.

demanded. How else were they to compete with the glass-walled new hotels that were going up, no matter how deficient these rivals might be in atmosphere, service, and above all, history?

For some, the challenges were simply too overwhelming and they gave up the fight, either closing altogether or replacing the old building with a new one on the same site, as happened with Tokyo's Imperial. Several continued to exist physically, but in such a state of disrepair and squalor that not even the most determined seeker of nostalgia would want to spend much time in them.

Others though, resisted extinction and gradually (very gradually in a few cases) realized that being historic might not necessarily be such a bad thing after all. Not all the new breed of travelers, it turned out, were so enchanted with contemporary accommodations. Indeed, quite a few of them were looking for just the sort of atmosphere the old hotels offered in abundance, even if it happened to be in a now unfashionable or inconvenient part of the city. Sometimes it turned out that a beguiling sense of history could be provided in buildings that were not hotels at all originally but still had architectural distinction. Thus Singapore's old post office became the elegant Fullerton, the former High Commissioner's stately residence in Kuala Lumpur became an all-suites retreat called the Carcosa and more than a few fairy-tale Indian palaces underwent extensive renovations and opened their doors to paying guests. Another successful strategy, pursued by many, was to add an ultra-modern wing while preserving all or most of the older sections and thus satisfying several tastes.

This wave of restorations and conversions began in the early 1980s, gained momentum in the 1990s and today extends through much of Asia, from India to China. The result, as seen on the following pages, is a collection of unique establishments where the past is not only present, but celebrated—and where one can discover what it was like to travel when a hotel was more than merely a collection of rooms and a restaurant or two.

Top: Painting of the original Oriental Hotel when it opened on Bangkok's Chao Phraya River in 1884. Designed by a local firm of Italian architects, it was the Thai capital's first grand hotel and, for many years, the only one.
Right: The Shiv Niwas Palace was formerly a royal guest house. Situated on a hill overlooking Udaipur, the Shiv Niwas offers spectaculat views of Lake Pichola.

THE PENINSULA
HONG KONG
ESTABLISHED 1928

The one constant aspect of Hong Kong, especially during the last few decades, has been the certainty of change. New skyscrapers have gone up, it seems, almost overnight, tunnels and bridges have replaced ferry boats, one by one even the most hallowed vestiges of British rule have given way to the never-ending need for more space and ever taller buildings. Among the few reminders of the old days that still stubbornly remain, overlooking the famous harbor from Kowloon, is the Peninsula Hotel.

"The Pen," as it has long been popularly known, was conceived in the early 1920s by the Kadoorie family, who originally came from Baghdad and established an extensive business empire. It eventually included the China Light and Power Company and family members were rewarded for their charitable work not only with knighthoods but also with the first Hong Kong peerage. At the time construction started, in 1922, the Trans-Siberian railway had just been completed, making it possible for an English traveler to book a train ticket all the way from London to the waterfront station at Kowloon. It was felt that the new six-story hotel should be a suitably grand establishment to greet these adventurous arrivals.

Progress was interrupted three years later when British troops were sent to Hong Kong for possible military action in China and, seeing that structural work on the Peninsula was almost complete, promptly requisitioned it as a temporary barracks. They stayed for 14 months and after they left it was necessary to replace not only the flooring but also all the bathtubs. Already a kind of survivor, the Peninsula finally opened its doors to paying guests on 11 December 1928.

Socially, it seemed at first to suffer from a disadvantage. The Governor lived on the island of Victoria, across the harbor, and so did most of the great merchants, whose mansions looked proudly down from the mountain there. Kowloon, by contrast, seemed remote and even a bit louche; according to Jan Morris in her book *Hong Kong*, old-fashioned ladies asked men, "Are you married or do you live in Kowloon?"

But the elegant Peninsula, with its ornate-columned and gilt-corniced lobby and luxurious guest rooms, helped change all that. Afternoon tea in the lobby became a ritual, the place where one ran into everybody who mattered. It also became the smartest place to give a dance or cocktail party, especially among the younger set, to drop in for lunch or a haircut and soon it was perhaps the best-known building in all of Hong Kong.

What few, if any, of these visitors suspected was that the manager of the barbershop was a spy, a naval commander no less, taking advantage of the informal atmosphere to gather military intelligence. This was revealed when the Japanese launched an attack on Hong Kong in December 1941; after a brief but spirited defense, the colony capitulated on Christmas Day, the surrender being signed at the Peninsula and the Governor being confined for two months in one of the hotel's suites before he was sent to a prison near Shanghai.

During the war years, the Peninsula was renamed the Toa and was reserved for Japanese officers and high-ranking dignitaries, while Hong Kong itself sank into misery and destitution. Half the population had gone by 1945, either by choice or forced to leave by the Japanese at an estimated rate of 23,000 a month throughout the occupation. When peace finally came, the once-bustling colony was in a sad state and, some felt, unlikely to ever recover.

They were spectacularly wrong. Within an amazingly short period of time, Hong Kong had regained its vigor and was on its way to scaling new economic heights that were previously unheard of. Newcomers poured in, both from foreign countries and also from mainland China after the Communist takeover in 1997. It became a unique phenomenon, immensely wealthy, glittering and in a state of almost constant change.

Meanwhile, the Peninsula continued to stand guard over the harbor, adapting to the new world in some ways, resisting it in others. Air conditioning was installed in the great, colonnaded lobby, but it remained a meeting place for world travelers, with the same diminutive bellboys and the same impeccable service. When a new, somewhat ugly Cultural Centre was built across the street in the early '90s, blocking the famous view, a 30-story tower was erected atop the old building, providing an additional 130 rooms (making a total of 300), a spa, two helipads and a Philippe Starck-designed restaurant offering a splendid, unrestricted panorama of Victoria and the port.

The hotel also has a fleet of Rolls-Royce limousines to ferry guests back and forth to Hong Kong's new airport, a helicopter service for those who want speed as well as style and a dazzling array of high-tech equipment in every room and suite.

Throughout 2003, the Peninsula celebrated its 75th anniversary with a series of gala events that reaffirmed its status as both a Hong Kong legend and an establishment still capable of taking on any would-be competitors.

Top: The Peninsula's lobby with its ornate columns and high ceilings. Soon after the hotel's opening in 1928, this became the most popular place in Hong Kong to meet for tea and cocktails.

Top right: A corner of the hotel's Spring Moon restaurant. The restaurant has a counter that serves over 25 types of Chinese tea.

Right: Archival photographs from the Peninsula's past adorn this wall in the hotel's business center. Not among them is the surrender of Hong Kong to the Japanese in 1941, which took place at the hotel.

Page 20: Hong Kong's Peninsula Hotel today. A modern tower wing was added to the original structure in the 1980s, preserving its famous view across the spectacular harbor.

Page 21: Art works like this bronze mythological tortoise and a collection of antique teapots add to the Chinese atmosphere of The Peninsula.

Top: The Peninsula's Philippe Starck-designed restaurant, Felix, is located on the 28th story of the hotel. Even the ultra-modern washroom, shown here, offers spectacular views of Victoria Harbour.

Below: From its stunning main dining area (**left**) to the ultra-modern Felix Bar (**right**), the Peninsula Hotel's Felix restaurant was designed to offer customers a truly glamorous dining experience. Restaurant magazine has ranked it among the top 50 restaurants in the world.

Right: The restaurant's dramatic curving stairway leads to the Felix Bar, which has quickly become one of the most popular hangouts in Hong Kong.

Opposite top: The Peninsula's swimming pool, ultra-modern in most ways but incorporating older traditions with the use of Roman-style pillars.

Left: When a waterfront building blocked the celebrated views of the harbor from much of the original structure, the Peninsula more than compensated with a 30-story tower boasting a swimming pool, spa and helipad. From the pool, guests can take in the full spectacle of Hong Kong's scenery. The pool features a retractable glass screeen that is closed when the weather turns cold.

Top: Decorative details that bring a touch of the classic past to even the most contemporary additions to the Peninsula, such as the intricate stuccowork (**left**) in the main lobby and the Roman-style pillar (**right**) in the swimming pool

Right: Rolls Royce limousines are available to transport guests to and from the airport or wherever they want to go around the city during their stay.

THE IMPERIAL
NEW DELHI, INDIA
ESTABLISHED 1936

In 1911, a year after his coronation, King-Emperor George V laid the foundations for New Delhi, which would replace Calcutta as the capital of India. It was to be no ordinary city but one that expressed, in the most monumental way imaginable, what the King's Private Secretary called "the power of Western civilization."

Sir Herbert Baker and Sir Edwin Lutyens were the architects of this greatest of Imperial projects, built on a hillock called Raisina outside the walls of Old Delhi, and it took more than 30 years to complete. A broad ceremonial boulevard called Kingsway led past the imposing Secretariat buildings, designed by Baker, to Lutyens' crowning achievement, the splendid Viceroy's palace. Bigger than Versailles, this amazing structure covered four and a half acres (one and a half hectares), had 12 courtyards, a vast hemispheric dome inspired by a Buddhist stupa and gardens that were partly in English style and partly in formal Moghul; it was staffed by close to 6,000 servants, of whom 400 were gardeners.

A city conceived on such a scale naturally called for a suitably grand hotel, and New Delhi acquired one in 1931, appropriately called the Imperial. Designed by D. J. Bromfield, one of Lutyens' associates, in a blend of Victorian and colonial styles with whimsical touches of art deco, the hotel occupied an eight-acre (three-hectare) site facing Queensway (now Janpath or "the Peoples Boulevard"), the main north-south artery. The hotel was luxuriously appointed with Italian marble, English silver and china, and European chandeliers, as well as a huge mirrored ballroom, where the Vicereine, Lady Willingdon, presided over the opening festivities.

Over the years that followed, under British rule and afterwards, the Imperial played host to a steady stream of distinguished visitors from all over the world, who either stayed in one of its over-sized suites, dined in one of its restaurants, or danced in the famous ballroom (which has springs beneath the flooring to reduce noise and bear the weight of 500 people).

By the early 1990s, however, it was beginning to show its age; a guide to India published in 1985 calls it "a haven of peace and relaxation amid city bustle" but also mentions "hideous floral carpets" and "reluctant air-conditioning." Its present owner, Jasdev Singh Akoi, therefore decided to embark on an ambitious five-year program of restoration and upgrading of facilities, aimed at incorporating the latest technology while preserving the hotel's unique historic flavor.

Some Indians, even today, have an ambivalent attitude about the colonial era, but Jasdev Singh Akoi is not one of them. He celebrates the Raj throughout the renovated Imperial by means of an extraordinary art collection assembled from many sources, from auction sales to princely palaces, and scattered about the hotel's 230 guest rooms, restaurants and public areas.

A few examples may suggest the nostalgic flavor of his choices. Emily Eden, a sister of Lord Aukland, Governor-General of India, came to visit in the 1830s and spent several months traveling around the subcontinent with him. In addition to a witty book of letters, *Up The Country*, Miss Eden produced several expert drawings of places and people, including a portrait of Maharaja Ranjit Singh, the "Lion of the Punjab," one of the most important people she and her brother met. The portrait now hangs on the third floor of the Imperial and both a suite and one of the hotel's choice meeting rooms are named after her.

There are works, too, by James Ferguson (1808–86), the leading authority on Indian architecture; James Bailie Fraser, whose subject was the Himalayas; Charles Stewart Hardinge (1822–94), who produced 26 lithographs entitled "Recollections of India"; and Anne Eliza Scott, an amateur artist who produced some charming views of Simla between 1850 and 1858.

1911, a restaurant and bar named for the year New Delhi's foundation stone was laid, is a veritable museum of Raj relics. There are old photographs and paintings of the great Durbar that celebrated the event, a spectacular 70-foot (21-meter) watercolor mural painted by A.P. Mongin around 1807, and cabinets displaying British regalia and awards for gallantry.

"One of the most arresting public displays of colonial images and memorabilia in all of Asia," Anthony Paul of *Fortune* magazine wrote of this vast collection, which is being catalogued in collaboration with the Smithsonian Museum of Washington.

Thanks to such priceless works of art, its award-winning restaurants, modern conveniences and an attentive staff of 657, the Imperial continues to maintain the high reputation it first established nearly 75 years ago.

Top: *A colonial atmosphere prevails in the Imperial's 1911 bar, named after the year New Delhi's foundation stone was laid.*

Left: *The door leading to the bar incorporates intriguing art deco details.*

Opposite top: *Daniell's Tavern, specializing in food from the Raj period, is named after an uncle and nephew team of engravers and painters who came to India in the late-18th century to record their impressions of the country. Many of their works have been collected by the Imperial's owner and are displayed here.*

Opposite bottom: *The San Gimignano is the Imperial Hotel's Italian restaurant and serves a wide variety of pasta dishes and premium Italian grappa and wines.*

Page 28: *The Imperial's lobby forms an impressive introduction to the rest of the hotel.*

Page 29: *The Imperial Hotel, on New Delhi's broad Kingsway boulevard, was designed in a blend of Victorian and colonial styles by an associate of Sir Edwin Lutyen, the great architect who was responsible for many of the city's most splendid edifices. Towering royal palms provide a stately touch to its spacious gardens.*

Left: The private dining terrace of the Royal Imperial Suite is one of the few areas of the hotel that still retain much of its original decor. The original black and white floor tiles remain although in the rest of the hotel, they have been exchanged for a softer look of beige and white.

Top: Potted palms, a breakfast table with wicker chairs and the black and white floor tiles help to retain the colonial feel of the Royal Imperial Suite.

Top: The Imperial's spacious Deco Suites are 650 square feet (60 square meters) in size and and derive their names from their art deco interiors.

Above: Paradiso DiVino is the name of the dining terrace in the hotel's Italian restaurant, the San Gimignano. The Paradiso DiVino's gazebos, trickling fountain and greenery create a very pleasant and relaxing ambiance for diners.

Left: Two identical vases guard the entrance to the private dining terrace in the Royal Imperial Suite. The suite is 2,100 square feet (195 square meters) in size and includes a steam room, sauna and Jacuzzi.

Right: This passageway on the second floor of the hotel defines the "new" *Imperial* after its extensive five-year renovation. In many sections of the hotel, beige and white tiles have replaced the more dramatic black and white ones that were so characteristic of British colonial architecture.

Below: The Lutyens' suites are named after Sir Edwin Lutyens, the architect who designed the Viceroy's palace in New Delhi and numerous other architectural wonders. The rooms are decorated with antique Raj furniture and art objects from the owner's extensive collection. The suite features marble baths, Fragonard & Bvlgari bathroom facilities, a four-poster king-size bed as well as modern facilities such as high speed wireless internet access and Bang & Olufsen televisions.

THE TAJ MAHAL
PALACE & TOWER
MUMBAI, INDIA
ESTABLISHED 1903

Some twenty-five years before the celebrated Gateway of India was erected on a spit of land called Apollo Bunder at the port of Bombay (now known as Mumbai), the first monument of the subcontinent that greeted arriving visitors by sea was the even more celebrated Taj Mahal Hotel.

This imposing structure, five stories tall and adorned with a huge glittering central dome as well as several smaller ones, had opened in 1903 and from that moment became what author Jan Morris called a synonym for the "quintessence of imperial amplitude."

The Taj was the ultimate achievement of one Jamsetji Nusserwanji Tata, the father of a Parsee dynasty who made his first fortune in the cotton trade and later branched out into mills, hydroelectric works, a shipping line and numerous other businesses. According to one story, Jamsetji took a foreign friend for dinner at a local hotel in the closing years of the 19th century and was denied entry simply because he was not European, a sadly familiar occurrence in those days when the British concept of racial superiority was at its zenith. Jamsetji, however, was in a position to respond: he decided to build a hotel so palatial Europeans would be attracted to it, but open it to Indians and people of all races.

Jamsetji went about the task with characteristic dedication. Two Indian architects, Sitaram Khanderao Vaidya and D.N. Mirza, drew up the original design and when Vaidya died, an English architect of radical persuasion, W. A. Chambers, took over the job. In 1898, foundations 40 feet (12 meters) deep were laid on two and a quarter acres (one hectare) of reclaimed land and on this rose a massive building flanked by two wings, creating space for a large courtyard. (Contrary to some reports, the U-shaped structure did not face the wrong way; the courtyard was created to trap late afternoon breezes, which blew not from the ocean but from a back bay and its position also ensured that most guests could enjoy rooms overlooking the sea.)

While the hotel was under construction, Jamsetji went to London, Dusseldorf, Berlin and Paris to select the furnishings, paying careful attention to every detail, from fabrics to lighting fixtures. In Paris he attended the opening of the Eiffel Tower and was inspired to order ten pillars of spun iron, which would hold up the ballroom of the Taj. Writing to his son Dorab about the decorations he commented: "In this matter, there is no science of taste established, though it is possible at some remote time such a universal agreement may be brought about. But taste in

this matter keeps so constantly varying that often fashions change every few years; and what goes out now, may come back. Under the circumstances, we must try to do what we think our customers would like."

Jamsetji died in 1904, but he had already seen the opening of his remarkable creation and the excitement it had stirred. Everything about the Taj, from its theatrical blend of architectural styles (Rajput and Gujerati, Florentine, Edwardian and Moorish) to its splendid atrium-style central stairwell and overall sense of space, was designed to impress; and this it most certainly did. As one visiting journalist wrote in 1905: "The Taj Hotel is on such a scale of magnificence and luxury that at first it rather took one's breath away."

It was the first commercial building in Bombay to be electrified, with its own power plant serving not only the rooms but also four lifts, a laundry and a Turkish bath. In addition, a gas-operated ice machine provided refrigeration and helped cool the suites. (It would later have Bombay's first licensed bar, its first restaurant to stay open all day, and its first discotheque.)

The hotel at once became Bombay's unrivaled social and political center. Banquets were held there twice for King George V and Queen Mary, once in 1905 before he was crowned and again in 1911 when he received his Indian subjects at a grand durbar. Another was held for Edward, Prince of Wales, when he visited in 1921. Even those anxious to put an end to British rule, among them Jawaharlal Nehru, Mohammed Ali Jinnah and Mahatma Gandhi were equally welcome, as was a steady stream of Maharajahs and Princes, for whom the Taj proved the perfect place to escape formality while still offering the palatial standards they were accustomed to. (The Maharajah of Patiala, for example, was able to check in with his entire retinue of staff, servants and personal harem and find rooms waiting for them all.)

The Taj maintained its lofty position and its fabled service through two world wars, the birth of Indian independence, and beyond. During World War II it became a 600-bed hospital, and later, in 1948, Lord Louis Mountbatten, the first governor general of independent India, chose it as the place to give his inaugural speech to the leaders of Indian industry.

Top: *This spacious swimming pool was added to the Taj Mahal during one of several expansions that began in the late 1960s. A dramatic statue of a lion shoots out a jet of water.*

Bottom: *Traditional Indian and European Art Deco elements, such as Hindhu carvings (left), wall lamps (middle) and the lion statue by the pool (right) were incorporated into the original hotel decorations.*

Right: *Elegant railings (top) and archways (bottom) give a light, airy effect in the original building. Inspired by the Eiffel Tower in Paris, the owner ordered ten columns of spun iron to support the hotel's ballroom.*

Page 36: *A staff member in traditional Indian dress stands outside the entrance of the legendary Taj Mahal in Mumbai, which has welcomed visitors since 1903.*

Page 37: *The imposing façade of the Taj Mahal, with its distinctive domes. Built by the father of a wealthy Parsee dynasty, it became one of India's most famous landmarks, featuring a blend of fanciful architectural styles and open to locals and foreigners.*

When King Ibn Saud of Saudi Arabia visited in 1956 and ordered a picnic lunch for 1,200 guests to take to the races, the hotel provided asparagus soup, paté de fois gras, smoked salmon, roast turkey, chicken, lamb, guinea-fowl, nine different salads, and four desserts.

It also kept pace with the modern world. A new floor, the sixth, was added in the late 1960s and a 23-story tower wing, designed by the American architect Melton Bekker, was added in the next decade. At the same time it branched out to create the Taj Group of Hotels, which now has 54 hotels in 39 locations across India with an additional 13 hotels overseas.

In the late 1990s, as the hotel's centenary drew near, both the old and new wings were completely renovated and refurbished. It was ready therefore to usher in the 21st century with an elaborate party on 17 January 2003, just as it had ushered in the 20th century in 1903.

Left: Dramatic supports for corridors and molded stucco decorations on archways and the ceiling contribute to the overall atmosphere of the hotel.

Top: The Taj Mahal offers generously appointed suites and rooms, each adorned with original paintings and period furniture that exude an aura of old-world charm and elegance.

Right: An Indian-style sofa and chair, with locally-made cushions, are features in this corner of the Rajput Suite. The suite has played host to many a celebrity and head of state and features a private balcony overlooking the Gateway of India.

Left: Interior of the enormous dome that is one of the most impressive features of the original building of the Taj Mahal, making it immediately visible to anyone arriving by sea. It was also the first commercial building in Bombay to be connected to the electrical power grid.

Top: The Taj Mahal combines Oriental, Florentine and Moorish architectural elements to create an elegant and visually striking hotel. The high vaulted ceiling, graceful archways and intricately-detailed railings help create a palatial splendor seldom seen in contemporary establishments.

Right: The intricate onyx columns and archway, stained glass panels and carved window panes are just a few examples of the level of detail and effort put into the Taj Mahal's design and construction.

THE OBEROI CECIL
SHIMLA, INDIA
ESTABLISHED 1884

The hill-stations of India, especially those in the Himalayan foothills of the north, were largely British creations. Beginning in the early 19th century, the colonial rulers wanted somewhere to escape the searing heat of the Indian summer, also perhaps to escape the demands of their often troublesome subjects, and they found it in those high enclaves where the weather and plant life comfortingly resembled those of home.

"Your hill-station was scarcely more than a village," Jan Morris wrote in her trilogy about the rise and fall of the Empire, "and was dwarfed by the scale of the country, but it had the startling impact of an intruder. It was definitely, gloriously out of place—a figure of despotic privilege. Where there should have been an eaved white temple with prayer flag up there, a Gothic steeple rose instead, with a weathercock on top and the white blobs of tombstones in the yard behind. Where one might expect the palace of Mir or Maharajah, a hotel in the Eastbourne manner stood, wicker chairs upon its terrace, awnings above its windows. There were military-looking buildings here and there, and genteel half-timbered villas disposed above rustic steps, and along the top of the ridge there ran a wide paved esplanade, with a bandstand, a fountain in a public garden, and benches, as on a promenade at home, surveying the Himalayan prospect."

The most famous of all these retreats was in Simla (now spelled Shimla and the capital of Himachal Pradesh state), perched on a mountain ridge 7,250 feet (2,200 meters) above sea level. The setting for Kipling's *Plain Tales from the Hills*, Simla was the summer capital of British India, where the Viceroy had an ornate palace at the top of Summer Hill and where for several months a year almost the entire government moved, along with countless family members. The trip itself was memorable, on a narrow-gauge railway that ran thrillingly for 60 miles (95 kilometers) and traversed 103 tunnels, 969 bridges and 900 curves before delivering its passengers to a magical destination with pine-scented air, a leisurely social life and spectacular scenery.

Some of the families had homes there, with very English names like "Strawberry Hill" and "Fair View" (the earliest, Kennedy Cottage, was built in 1822), and many retired to Simla's invigorating climate after their work was done rather than return to the now-strange land of their birth. For visitors there were several hotels, of which one of the most popular was

the Cecil, known as the finest hotel in north India for its comforts and colonial grandeur.

The Cecil opened in 1884 and for the remaining years of British rule its spacious rooms were crowded at the height of the summer season with a mixture of civil servants and their families, young military men on leave, and occasional tourists making a grand tour of India. There were picnics in the Glen, bracing walks through forests of cedar and pine, amateur performances at the Gaiety Theatre (where Kipling was once booed off the stage), shopping excursions to the bazaar and for a select few individuals, invitations to dine and dance at Viceroy House. It was not uncommon for romances to blossom in such pleasant settings, and occasionally there were scandals to enliven the generally bucolic atmosphere (indeed, a favorite destination on promenades was Scandal Point).

Hill stations like Simla inevitably suffered a momentary decline after independence came to India but as it turned out, sophisticated Indians were just as eager as their former rulers to enjoy such novelties as chilly air and open fireplaces and were just as willing to make the effort to journey to places that offered them such niceties. Consequently, many of the old hotels were bought by new owners and given makeovers that brought them into the top ranks of international resort facilities.

After a period of neglect, the Cecil was acquired by the prestigious Oberoi group and lovingly restored and expanded; it reopened in 1997 with 79 rooms and suites. In addition to the original Tudor Wing, there is a new five-story Cecil Wing with a lofty atrium, both with sweeping views of forested hills stretching off into the distance to the snow-capped Himalayas. Furnishings include custom-made sofas, chairs and wardrobes in the spirit of the Cecil's past, while other amenities include two restaurants, an indoor swimming pool, a billiard room, a fitness center and a children's center offering supervised activities as well as special meals.

The peak season in Shimla, as it was in British days, is between April and June, but it has now become almost as popular in the winter months of November and December. At either time, jackets and sweaters are welcome in the evening, cheery fires encourage cozy gatherings and public gardens display a rich profusion of exotic flowers unknown to the plains far below. The little railway running up from Kalka, shut down for a number of years, resumed service in November 2003, further adding to the nostalgia of a visit.

Top: View of the Cecil's bar, which has comfortable leather-covered armchairs and tall lamps to create an intimate mood for guests after a walk in the bracing air of the hill-station.

Page 44: A close-up of a table setting in one of the Cecil's restaurants. The Cecil is renowned for offering guests a fine dining experience.

Page 45: The multi-level lobby of the Oberoi Cecil has been a convivial gathering spot for visitors to Simla since it opened in the mid-1920s. Shown here is the atrium lounge where guests can enjoy a quiet drink. The hotel was tastefully restored and expanded when it was taken over by the Oberoi group in the 1990s.

Top: A cosy corner in one of the suite rooms. A period writing table, a lamp and a carved wooden art nouveau chair makes this rather eclectic collection work together nicely.

Right: The imposing main stairwell has helped well-coiffed ladies and well-dressed gentlemen make their grand entrance into the main lobby or dining room.

Bottom: Sofas and cushions covered in luxurious Indian textiles are one of the hallmarks of the Oberoi Hotels. Lamps and period paintings help recreate a colonial atmosphere. Corners such as these allowed guests to relax without being approached by waiters. Although if one needed to be served afternoon tea or a quiet drink it was easily arranged.

Top: Jacuzzis, internet access and a business center were just some of the modern features added when the Cecil was restored.

Left: The Cecil's dining room has vents in the wall to provide cool air in the summer and warmth in the cooler months .

Right: The hotel's heated indoor swimming pool offers stunning views of the Himalayas and the pine forests around Shimla. The Cecil sits at an elevation of over 7,000 feet (2,100 meters), making this one of the highest indoor pools in the world.

SHIV NIWAS
PALACE
UDAIPUR, INDIA
ESTABLISHED 1900

Situated on a hill overlooking Udaipur's Lake Pichola, where the fabled Lake Palace Hotel seems to float like an ethereal dream, the Shiv Niwas formerly served as the royal guest house at the southern end of the vast, sprawling Shambhu Palace complex. The crescent-shaped structure, with carved pillars, wall paintings and shimmering ponds, was built in a blend of Mughal and Rajput architectural styles in the late 19th century and used as a residence by the Maharana Fateh Singh, one of the most colorful (and, to the British, difficult) Rajput rulers.

Born in 1849, Fateh Singh came from a rustic background and was essentially uneducated. Nevertheless, his noble bearing and aura of austere self-assurance so impressed the ruling Maharana, Sajjan Singh, who had no heir, that he adopted Fateh as his son and successor. He was 32 when he began his long reign, which lasted 46 years and more than confirmed Sajjan's confidence in him.

A contemporary chronicler glorified his Fateh as being "one of the most courteous of courtly Rajputs, an unfailing product of high culture and refinement, intensely conservative... a typical Rajput of the old school, a keen sportsman, taking delight in all manly sports of the Rajputs, a daring huntsman ever on the track of big game... He spends his days usefully in the task of governing his people on old traditional lines of personal rule and takes a personal interest in the details of administration in the welfare of his people. He is liked by his own subjects, respected by other Rajput princes and their subjects and is second to none in his dignified loyalty to the Imperial Throne of Britain."

Not all the British rulers would have agreed with the last part of this assessment though, for Maharana Fateh Singh tolerated their presence with a lofty reluctance that he demonstrated on several famous occasions.

In 1903, when the Viceroy, Lord Curzon, held a durbar in Delhi to celebrate the coronation of King Edward VII, Fateh came in two trains, accompanied by a thousand retainers. Unfortunately for Lord Curzon, Fateh returned to Udaipur without disembarking when he discovered he had not been according his rightful place in the procession. He did the same thing again in 1911 when King George V and Queen Mary came for another, even more important Delhi durbar.

The final straw for the British seems to have come in 1921 when the Prince of Wales made a special trip to Udaipur to see him. The Maharana, pleading illness, refused to meet him at the railway station and sent his son, Bhupal, instead. The British reacted swiftly to this perceived slight, deposing Fateh on the grounds that he was too inflexible and was ignorant of the social unrest being stirred up by a new communist movement in the region. The British allowed Fateh to retain titular right to the throne but effectively handed power to Bhupal, who succeeded Fateh when he died in 1930.

Maharana Bhupal Singh used the Shiv Niwas Palace for entertaining royal guests. The single-story palace originally had nine suites around the courtyard. One was adorned with beautiful paintings and the others with inlaid glass mosaics. One suite contained a collection of crystal furniture and objets d'art from England, which had been ordered by Fateh's father but which arrived after his death; Fateh, however, never used it and it remained in crates until Bhupal's reign.

It was another Maharana, Bhagwat Singh, who conceived the idea of turning the palace into a hotel in 1982. This was twenty-odd years after he had done the same thing with the exquisite Lake Palace and the work was continued by his son and heir Arvind Singh. More suites were added on a second floor overlooking the courtyard, as well as a marble swimming pool and a conference room. The traditional decorations of the older suites have been carefully preserved and all the rooms display a rich collection of Persian carpets, ivory-inlaid furniture, Mewar School miniature paintings, colored chandeliers, Chinese lampshades and family portraits, all discovered in the royal godowns by Elizabeth Kerker, the noted interior designer Bhagwat Singh hired to oversee the renovation.

Louis Rousselet, a French traveler in the late 1870s, attended a banquet at the palace and left a record of the experience. The dinner, he wrote, "is quite in the European style and the wine, which comes from the royal cellars, is first rate. The [Maharana] receives his guests but only waits till they are seated at the table, considering that, as his religion forbids him from taking part in our repast, his presence as a spectator would be a restraint upon his guests. Numerous toasts soon remove all constraint, and the Rajpoots [sic] and Europeans vie with each other in doing honor to the wines of the West and to the Manila and Havana cigars."

Guests today at the Shiv Niwas still find a similar mixture of hospitality, opulence and modern comforts in a setting that recalls the bygone days of princely rule in Rajasthan.

Opposite top: An attendant in a typical Rajput outfit in one of the Shiv Niwas courtyards.

Left: An evening view of the palace, with its blend of architectural styles and general opulent splendor.

Top: Crenallated walls and Moghul-influenced décor characterize the guest room exteriors in Shiv Niwas. Lacy wrought iron furniture adds to the effect of a Moghul-inspired fantasy although for the generations of Maharajahs who have occupied this imposing fortress palace, it is an everyday reality.

Above: The afternoon sun casts shadows against the sun-pinkened walls of the Shiv Niwas. The ancient door is a typical feature of Rajasthan palaces.

Page 50: A pierced wood gate leads into one of the courtyards at the Shiv Niwas Palace, which was transformed into a hotel in 1982 and thus allowed modern travelers to experience the magical world of Rajput royalty.

Page 51: Formerly a royal guest house, the Shiv Niwas overlooks Lake Pichola and was built in the late 19th century in a mixture of Moghul and Rajput styles.

Top: The Moghul domes of Shiv Niwas and the huge Shambhu Palace complex, an impressive example of Rajput architecture, rise amid the thickly-forested hills of Udaipur.

Bottom: Looking up at the western facing outer wall of the imposing Shiv Niwas. Circular towers afford better views of the nearby Lake and the jutting covered balconies afford comfortable sitting places, that you can never get in a conventional square room.

Right: A marble floor and Moorish archways lead to a terrace overlooking Lake Pichola.

Bottom right: Lacy ironwork provides an elegant frame for al fresco dining or a languid breakfast on the balcony of one of the luxurious guest rooms.

Bottom: Persian carpets, family portraits and distinctive furniture is used in guest suites. The English designer hired for the renovation of the Shiv Niwas found many of the items in the royal godowns where they had remained unpacked for years.

Left: *Curving walls decorated with painted motifs, a bed in an imposing canopied structure and a huge crystal chandelier make this master suite a memorable experience for guests.*

Top: *Black and white checkered tiles were a favorite of both the British Raj and the Rajasthan Maharajahs. This front terrace in one of the original guest rooms makes an elegant counterpoint to the curving period French furniture—no doubt a gift from some visiting VIP. The bevelled and cut mirrors are another feature than can be seen in many of the grand residences and palaces of the desert state.*

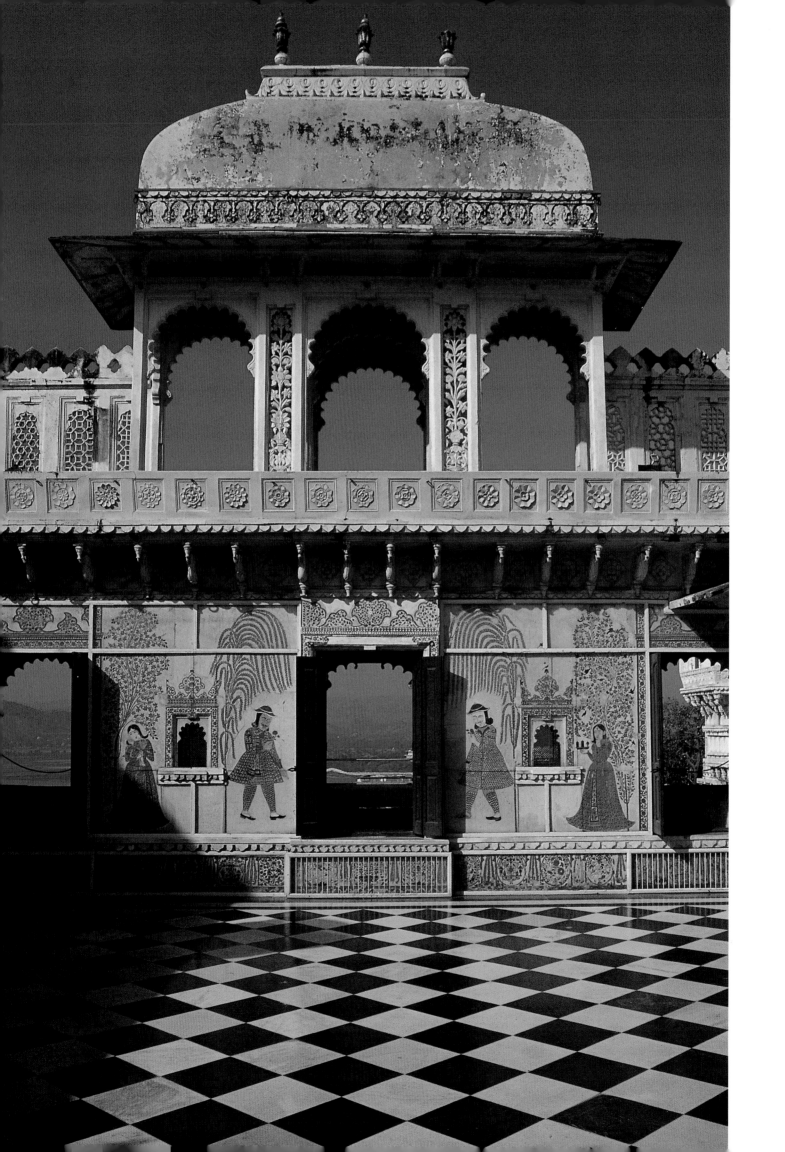

Left: An elegantly-proportioned gateway on one of the palace terraces, decorated with paintings of figures in traditional Rajput dress.

Top: Tables set for an open-air dinner party recall the days when the Shiv Niwas was used for entertaining royal guests.

Bottom: As evening falls, the palace and Lake Pichola in the background acquire a magical atmosphere.

TAJ LAKE PALACE
UDAIPUR, INDIA
ESTABLISHED 1746

Thanks to its appearance as a memorable setting in such films as the James Bond action-thriller *Octopussy* and the epic television series based on Paul Scott's *Jewel in the Crown*, countless people who have never been to India are familiar with the magical beauty of this white marble palace that seems to float serenely on the azure waters of Lake Pichola in Udaipur, Rajasthan.

The state of Rajasthan, which has been described as "classic fantasy India at its best," is famous for the extravagant lifestyles once enjoyed by its princes and for the fairy-tale palaces they erected in each of its major cities. Udaipur, the capital of Mewar state from 1567, had the largest of them all, a masterpiece of Rajput architecture over a mile and a half long overlooking Lake Pichola; but it is better known for the smaller Lake Palace, conceived as a private retreat and accessible only by boat.

Also known as Jag Niwas (Abode of Jag), the Lake Palace was built by Maharana Jagat Singh II, sixtieth prince of the Mewar Dynasty, who ruled Udaipur for 17 years. The foundations were laid in 1743 and the palace, covering an area of about four acres (one and a half hectares) and including gardens, lotus pools and courtyards, was completed three years later. Here in his own secluded paradise, away from the formal ceremonies of his main residence, the Maharana could spend his leisure hours with the ladies of his court, while according to legend potential intruders were deterred by crocodiles that lived in the surrounding water. (Another story tells of one bold courtesan who claimed she could dance across the lake on a thin rope; the Maharana wagered half his kingdom on this feat and then, when it seemed likely she might succeed, cut the rope so that she fell to her death.)

Like other states in Rajasthan, Udaipur came under British control in the early decades of the 19th century though it managed to resist almost any cultural influences from the new rulers, just as it had resisted the earlier Moghul invaders. (Its Maharanas refused to go to the Moghul city of Delhi to demonstrate their opposition and only did so after it became the capital of a newly independent India.)

Even after independence in 1947 and the eventual loss of their titles and revenues, the royal families of the region still retained their vast palaces. Keeping such buildings up in anything like their former splendor, however, proved an increasingly difficult task, and a number of owners began to put them to more practical and profitable uses.

In 1959, the Maharana Bhagwat Singh conceived the idea of turning the Lake Palace into a hotel so that paying guests could enjoy its unique attractions. Renovation work (which would go on fitfully for more than 20 years) was still underway in 1962 when the American ambassador John Kenneth Galbraith arrived as escort to Jacqueline Kennedy, who was on a tour of India with her sister. They were housed in the main palace, "a vast marble affair," but made a private excursion around the lake and to the future hotel, which made a great impression. "If carried through according to present plans," Galbraith wrote in his journal, "it will be one of the most charming in the world. It has lovely intimate courtyards and the walls are decorated with inlaid glass of superb workmanship."

A year later, in February, the work was still incomplete but Galbraith nevertheless had the pleasure of attending the official opening of the new hotel. He also took a boat trip around Pichola Lake, where he noted "a great variety of water fowl" as well as some enormous crocodiles; the latter, he wryly observed, "are a priceless asset for they will greatly discourage water skiing."

"Built for pleasure, now run for pleasure," as one travel writer described it, the Lake Palace has been under the management of the prestigious Taj Group since 1971. During renovations, priority was given to restoring the exquisite glass inlay panels, as well as the carved marble columns and filigreed screens, mural paintings and stained-glass windows in major suites and pools and fountains scattered about the complex. In addition to 85 rooms, including 13 suites and 53 deluxe rooms, the hotel also includes restaurants, jewelry shops and landscaped formal gardens. Boats may be hired for trips around the lake and visits to the royal guest house (Shiv Nivas), the rambling City Palace, and the treasure-filled bazaars on the mainland.

The dancing girls may be gone, but few experiences in today's well-traveled world can compare with enjoying a romantic sundowner on one of the Lake Palace's marble terraces, watching the golden light slowly fade over the water and faraway hills.

Top: "Built for pleasure, now run for pleasure," as one brochure describes the Lake Palace, the enchanting structure has been used as a setting in numerous films and television programs.

Right: A swimming pool with a striking inlaid design, overlooking the blue water of Lake Pichola, is one of the more modern additions to the hotel.

Page 60: A brass urn sits atop an ornate table—a sweet decorative feature in one of the more luxurious suites. Wispy curtains soften the glare of the afternoon sun and the view out to the Lake.

Page 61: Dating from the mid-18th century, the Lake Palace was one of the first examples of royal Rajput architecture to be converted into a hotel for tourists. The renovation of the palace extended over nearly two decades.

Left: *A lounge with graceful columns and furnishing in soft, soothing colors adds to the general effect of airy lightness.*

Bottom left: *Flower petals and aromatic candles add to the restful atmosphere of the spa at the Lake Palace; the royal palace on the mainland can be seen in the background.*

Right: *A waiter lights the candles in preparation for dinner guests at specially-laid tables in the softly illuminated garden of the Lake Palace. The candles and other lights add an ethereal and romantic effect to the ordered garden.*

Bottom: *A guest suite is furnished with numerous Rajput antiques and handicrafts, while sitting areas offer views of the lake and its changing moods.*

Top: An antique brass vessel and a Rajput painting are displayed in a niche above a curving sofa, while ancient weapons adorn the walls along with decorative frescoes and moldings.

Clockwise from opposite top left: A cushioned seating area runs along the wall of this gorgeous marble lined suite. Afternoon sun streams through the windows illuminating the lavish cushions and polished silver ice bucket. Carved white marble columns help define the seating space—no doubt once a favored evening haunt of a long gone Maharajah and his women; On the terrace between suites this niche looks almost heavenly in the evening light. Carved marble and plaster help to create a feeling of richness and grandeur; Afternoon light bounces off the lake to filter in through this finely carved marble tree of life and an intimate seating corner designed to lounge and relax—the antithesis of the more formal British approach to relaxation; Walls with mozaic artwork and comfortable leather armchairs make for a particularly pleasing spot to while away a few hours.

DWARIKA'S HOTEL
KATHMANDU, NEPAL
ESTABLISHED 1964

Certain countries in Asia lacked easy access by railway or sea and thus long remained off the traditional route for even the most adventurous travelers. This was particularly true of the land-locked kingdoms at high altitudes, which came under no direct control by any of the colonial powers. Such places were not only difficult to reach but often dangerous, and while a few daunt-less explorers and mountain climbers occasionally ventured into them, they remained virtually unknown to other visitors. This would not change until the advent of mass air travel.

In December 1968, a Thai International jet landed at Kathmandu in Nepal. It was not the first aircraft to provide a service to the lofty Himalayan kingdom. DC-3s belonging to Indian, Royal Nepal and Pakistan Airlines were already offering a way into the remote valley, which remained unconnected by road to the outside world as late as 1955. A handful of adventurous travelers (about seven a day) were already beginning to discover Nepal's numerous monasteries, narrow streets and breathtaking panorama of snow-capped peaks. But the Thai International flight opened a new age of mass tourism and suddenly Nepal became a favored destination not only for Nirvana-seeking backpackers but also for more ordinary visitors as well.

Considering its relative isolation and the lack of a thriving tourism industry at the time, it is not really surprising that Kathmandu had never been able to boast the sort of landmark hotel that could be found in other major cities in the region. All that was about to change, however. Indeed, the beginnings of one can be traced back to even before the first outsiders discovered Nepal.

Dr. Tony Hagen, an anthropologist and author of the first book on Nepal, published in 1950, has described how it evolved. "In 1952," he writes, "the late Dwarika Das Shrestha was out jogging when he came upon some carpenters sawing off the carved portion of an intricately engraved wood pillar. It had been part of an old building which had been torn down to make room for a modern structure; amidst the rubble lay the bits and pieces of exquisitely carved woodwork several centuries old, ready to be carted off as firewood."

Proud of his country's rich cultural heritage, he was so shocked by this careless desecration that he impulsively gave the carpenters new lumber for their fires and took the old pillar away with him. Collecting such carvings became first a hobby and later a lifetime passion. By 1964, he had enough to decorate a Nepalese-style brick building, which he built in his garden, and this eventually grew into what was first called the Village Hotel and is now Dwarika's Hotel.

Dwarika Das Shrestha died in 1992. Before that, he had started a "heritage workshop" in 1972 to produce replica woodcarvings that were faithful in every detail to the originals. He also launched a travel agency and the hotel full of Nepalese products, from furniture and art objects to hand-woven textiles and elegant lighting fixtures. Dwarika's wife Ambica and his daughter Sangita, who also shared his obsession with Nepal's ancient crafts, continued his work and later expanded the hotel to its present form.

Originally, Dwarika's had only 30 large, comfortable rooms, each of which was individually designed, plus a staff of 150 who worked either in the hotel or in the restoration workshop. When the cost of good timber rose to prohibitive costs during construction, Dwarika Das developed a way of achieving the same effect on the front walls with terra cotta bricks, now widely used on other Kathmandu buildings. In 1998, two luxury wings were added to the hotel, adding another 39 rooms displaying the same wealth of traditional craftsmanship.

The textiles and carpets are all locally produced, while terra cotta sculptures from Hindu and Buddhist mythology look out from niches in the walls.

Dwarika Das Shrestha's desire to preserve his country's ancient culture has resulted in a truly unique hotel that not only delights foreign visitors but also constitutes a living model for other Nepalese who wish to create similar works of art.

Top: Water spills into a swimming pool through spouts adorned with Nepalese figures. The main building behind is in traditional style once common in Kathmandu.

Top right: A sitting room at Dwarika's, with traditional furniture made by local craftsmen, handwoven textiles covering cushions and assorted Nepalese objects.

Far right: A bed draped with a mosquito net adds to the period flavor of the hotel's rooms.

Right: A bath in one of the guest rooms, embellished with flower petals and burning votive candles. Such attention to detail has made Dwarika's a favorite among world-weary travelers.

Page 68: Detail of one of the finely wrought bronze lamps that can be found in abundance in various parts of Dwarika's Hotel.

Page 69: Dwarika's Hotel began in the 1950s when Dwarika Das Shresta began collecting examples of Nepal's rich cultural heritage, then being discarded in favor of more modern structures. Many of the furnishings in the lobby and guest rooms were products of a "heritage workshop" which he established before his death in 1992 to continue Nepalese traditions.

Far left: Framed black and white photographs of VIP visitors to Kathmandu over the decades are arranged on the walls of the upstairs bar, adding a rakish charm to this delightful sitting area.

Left: Nepalese-style jar made into a lamp and cushions with geometric patterns are among the items that reflect local culture.

Right: The dazzling red-orange flowers of a flame vine form a burst of seasonal color on the rustic roof tiles.

Left: The courtyard, surrounded by traditional buildings, stands in marked contrast to the surrounding world of modern Kathmandu, thus fulfilling the dream of Dwarika's founder.

Right: Terra-cotta sculptures of figures from Hindu mythology are displayed throughut the hotel compound.

ANANDA
IN THE HIMALAYAS
TEHRI GARHWAL, INDIA
ESTABLISHED 1911

Spectacular scenery, beguilingly ornate old palace buildings and modern facilities are combined to create a memorable atmosphere in several of India's more recently established hotels. Few places, however, achieve this fusion more successfully than the Ananda, a 100-acre (40 hectare) resort in the state of Uttaranchai, which overlooks the Rishikesh Valley, the Ganges River, and the forested foothills of the mighty Himalayas soaring in the distance.

The older structures consist of the 19th-century palace of the Maharajah of Tehri Garhwal and a sumptuously restored Viceregal Lodge that was built in 1911, the year of the famous Delhi Durbar attended by King George V and Queen Mary at which it was announced that India's official capital would be moved from Calcutta to New Delhi. An expected visit from the Viceroy of the time unfortunately failed to materialize, but the splendid lodge remains, along with the Maharajah's palace, to serve as an exotic reception center for guests on their way to more modern spa facilities beyond.

The palace is predominately Moorish in style, with added accents of Italian Renaissance and Rajasthani while the adjacent lodge has Indian Bijapuri arches on the outside and an Art Deco interior. Guests are welcomed in the reception hall of the lodge, on one side of which is a splendid lounge with two original fireplaces (a most welcome sight given the cold temperatures), Venetian crystal chandeliers, a 14-foot (four-meter) high ceiling made of stamped and pressed copper and photographs of such figures as Queen Elizabeth (signed in 1937) and the last British Viceroy, Lord Louis Mountbatten. On one side of the hall is a billiards room, which has a 150-year-old handcarved billiards table and the Maharajah's original cues. On the other side is the Maharajah's library, containing his collection of over 1,000 rare books on ancient medicinal sciences, a subject in which he took a keen personal interest and that now serves as the main attraction for most of Ananda's visitors.

A grand staircase with Burmese teak banisters and newel posts leads from the reception area to the spacious Viceregal Suite, which offers panoramic views of the landscape as well as a host of contemporary amenities including a Jacuzzi overlooking the Rishikesh valley and palace gardens and a private elevator for occupants of the suite.

Other guests proceed from the Viceregal Lodge to an area consisting of a sports and spa complex that includes an amphitheatre for entertainment, a lounge and restaurant, and 75 deluxe rooms and suites built on five levels down a slope. Indigenous materials have been used wherever possible, and the rooms are furnished in a subtle blend of stylish comfort and serenity, each with its own private balcony from which to savor the scenery. A restaurant surrounded by a tree-top deck serves a delectable choice of Ayurvedic, Asian and Western cuisine prepared by a chef with years of experience and a particular interest in developing distinctive Ananda spa dishes.

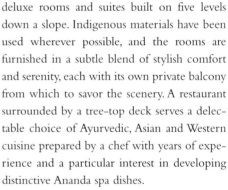

As the Maharajah's library suggests, Ananda is dedicated to the physical and mental well-being of its guests through a holistic approach that combines Eastern and Western healing principles. The spa features 20 therapy rooms, a heated swimming pool and hydrotherapy facilities. It also offers consultation services related to the ancient Indian Ayurveda system, wellness, lifestyle and general fitness so that programs designed to meet individual needs can be recommended. Personalized yoga and meditation sessions conducted by resident instructors are also available. For those who want a more adventurous stay, river rafting on the Ganges, trekking and visits to the Rajaji and Chilla national parks can be arranged.

The Ananda in the Himalayas is one of India's most distinctive resorts, offering either a comprehensive approach to better health and spiritual rejuvenation or merely a magical place to relax and escape the stressful pressures of the outside world.

Opposite top: A broad curving staircase adds an imposing grandeur to the beautifully designed and award-winning Spa at Ananda in the Himalayas.

Left: The lavishly decorated yet cosy reception room boasts a Venetian crystal chandelier and one of two original fireplaces that provide warmth on cooler evenings.

Top left to right: Once part of the Maharajah's residence, the old wing of the Ananda is now the most elegant and sought after part of the hotel; Outside the meeting room, a long table and portrait of a cheetah make an interesting design feature; The long table in the meeting room can also be used for special dinners and functions.

Page 74: Built in 1911 to accommodate a Viceroy who never arrived, this was part of the palace of the Maharaja of Tehri Garhwal; today, it serves as a reception area for visitors who come for spa treatments.

Page 75: The heated outdoor lap pool of the spa complex, overlooking the Rishikesh Valley, the holy river Ganges, and the foothills of the lofty Himalaya mountain range.

Left: View from an upper terrace, proving a panoramic view of the valley below and the Himalayan mountains in the background.
Right: This section of the hotel leads to the main complex of the Maharajah of Garhwal's palace, a splendidly-preserved piece of colonial architecture that is still maintained by the Maharajah.
Bottom: Soft feathery bamboo plants define the entrance to the hotel's restaurant, simply known as the Restaurant. The Restaurant's recipes are prepared according to Ayurvedic principles of cooking balanced and healthy meals.
Bottom right: Flowers placed in bowls with candles add an intimate decorative touch throughout the Ananda. Small touches such as this separate the world's best hotels from the merely good ones.

Clockwise from left: An assistant prepares one of the Ayurvedic treatment rooms at the spa. Ayurvedic treatments are just a part of the huge menu of spa treatments which even includes a range of skin care products, that are available in this first class spa; The relaxing Jacuzzi room looks out to the garden and beyond to the forests that surround Rishikesh; An imposing compass-like decoration is the main feature in the spa entrance.

Right: Golden stalks of bamboo and earth-colored stones add a tropical touch just outside the entrance to one of the Ananda Spa's treatment rooms.

Bottom: The façade of the Viceregal Lodge, which is the first view visitors have when they arrive at the spa.

Page 80: The cool mountain air and surrounding greenery at Ananda in the Himalayas are ideal for such therapeutic activities as meditation.

GALLE
FACE HOTEL
COLOMBO, SRI LANKA
ESTABLISHED 1864

"This is really an imposing-looking hotel, and, I fancy, a very comfortable one. Harry and I have two large, high-studded, airy rooms en suite, mine with three large windows with sun hoods painted white." Thus a well-to-do American woman named Clara Kathleen Rogers wrote in her journal in 1903. She was on an Asian odyssey with her husband and two friends, they had just arrived in Sri Lanka from India and the hotel where they, like so many others, were staying was the already venerable Galle Face, with sweeping views of the sea just outside.

The Galle Face opened for business in 1864, more than ten years before either the Oriental in Bangkok or Raffles in Singapore and thus qualifies as the oldest of all Asia's grand hotels. Facing the sea and adjacent to Galle Face Green, which used to be a race course, the rambling three-story structure epitomizes the sort of atmosphere world travelers expected when they wandered through the tropics in the late 19th and early 20th centuries. With its lofty ceilings and slowly turning fans, endless verandahs, barefoot servants always at hand and palm trees rustling in breezes just outside, it is incomparable. ("I shall never have a better chance to study the anatomy of the coconut tree than now," wrote Mr. Rogers. "I look from my windows, I see nothing else, except the Pompeian red road and the sea.")

The guest register constitutes a who's who of just about every notable person who has passed through Sri Lanka, or Ceylon as it was known until 1972. Mark Twain, for example, arrived in 1896 on a round-the-world lecture tour that he hoped would solve the bankruptcy into which imprudent business ventures had plunged him. He stopped only a few days and like most visitors was dazzled by the beauty of the island and its people: "The drive through the town and out to the Galle Face by the seashore, what a dream it was of tropical splendors of bloom and blossom and Oriental conflagrations of costume! The walking groups of men, women, boys, girls, babies—each individual was a flame, each group a house afire for color... And all harmonious, all in perfect taste; never a discordant note; never a color on any person swearing at another color on him or failing to harmonize faultlessly with the colors of any group the wearer might join."

Though unrecorded, no doubt similar sentiments were felt by other famous guests like Lord Louis Mountbatten, who stayed there when he came down from his headquarters in the botanical gardens at Kandy during World War II; Noel Coward, another wartime visitor who gave a show for Allied troops,

Alec Guinness who filmed *The Bridge on the River Kwai*; and perhaps even troubled Vivien Leigh, who suffered a nervous breakdown while making another film called *Elephant Walk*.

One who liked Sri Lanka so much he ended up spending the rest of his life there was science-fiction author Sir Arthur Clarke. Even after moving to his own home, Clarke kept in touch with K.C. Kuttan, a dignified man with a huge white moustache who served as the Galle Face's doorman, and attended the party given in 2002 to celebrate Kuttan's 60 years of dedicated service.

Under legendary chairman Cyril Gardiner, who took over in 1966, the Galle Face maintained its high standards and upgraded its facilities long after the British Raj departed. The bitter civil war that started in the 1980s and steep drop in the tourist numbers inevitably took their toll. Simon Winchester, a writer for *Condé Nast Traveller* in the mid-1990s, lamented these developments and expressed fears for the future. The Galle Face, he thought, was a very special place with "mighty entrance halls; vats of water with hundreds of swirling rose petals; notices beside the ancient elevators inviting nervous guests to walk up and down the stairs, waiters who seem to have been standing on the same spot, beside the same potted palm, for half a century; the swimming pool right beside the Indian Ocean, so that during the monsoon you get drenched by the breakers even if you don't elect to bathe. The place is far too pleasingly primeval... ever to be modernized. It must not become an expensive and ersatz version of its early self, refurbished into a parody."

After resisting change for some 140 years however, The Galle Face suddenly faced up to the need for renovation. It opened an 85-room Regency Wing, as well as a spacious spa and several new restaurants. Simon Winchester will be happy, though, to know that the original rooms, the splendid lobby and seaside verandah, though spruced up a bit, remain much the same as they always were.

Clockwise from opposite top left: Tables set for dinner along one of the hotel's verandahs, cooled by ceiling fans just as in its old days; The hallway that leads out to the divine balconies that overlook the sea and to the suites at the end. White light and space are the defining characteristics of this most majestic of hotels; A guest relaxes on one of the Galle Face's numerous verandahs, overlooking coconut palms along the beach.

Clockwise from top: A bartender polishes glasses at the main lobby bar; A low-rise building with red-tiled roofs and breezy verandahs, the hotel set a pattern for many other grand hotels in the tropics; The characteristic black and white checkerboard tiles are used to great effect on the main lawn of the Galle Face Hotel. Looking out to the Indian Ocean this area has played host to generations of elegant cocktail parties. Most of the VIP guests who visit Sri Lanka have stopped by or stayed at this hotel.

Page 84: Windows at the Galle Face offer enticing views of the sea.

Page 84: Towering carved doors at the entrance of the Galle Face, one of Asia's oldest hotels. The sprawling structure has been a prominent feature of Colombo's seafront since the middle of the 19th century.

Opposite top: *Evening view of the hotel with palms and fragrant frangipani trees. "I shall never have a better chance to study the anatomy of the coconut tree than now," wrote a guest who stayed there in 1903.*

Opposite bottom: *Terrace overlooking the sea at sunset, one of the most popular gathering spots at the Galle Face.*

Left: *A member of the Galle Face's staff welcomes guests.*

Bottom: *A guest room, with simple but comfortable furniture that recalls a long-ago age of travel.*

MOUNT LAVINIA HOTEL
SRI LANKA
ESTABLISHED 1806

Legends abound in Sri Lanka, so perhaps it is inevitable that one of the island's most celebrated beauty spots should have its own. Thus it is said the original builder of what became the Mount Lavinia Hotel was Sir Thomas Maitland, a Lieutenant General with the East India Company, who came to Ceylon, as the island was then known, as the appointed Governor in 1805. He was 46, still unmarried and described by one biographer as "a great human force." He was not immune to feminine charms however, and shortly after he arrived he fell in love with a local girl.

Her name was Lovina Aponsuwa and she was a dancer of notable beauty, though being of mixed Portuguese and Sinhala blood she was far below Sir Thomas' exalted station. Nevertheless she captured his heart and soon he began to look for a discreetly situated location where he could build a residence without incurring the approbation of his fellow countrymen.

He was particularly drawn to a headland on the Western coast known as Galkissa (a name that was possibly derived from Gal-vissa, or "twenty boulders"), not far from the present capital of Colombo, which happened to be the only elevated site overlooking a beautiful bay. Here he erected a mansion described as "handsomely built, laid out in mahogany and calamander wood," with white columns, polished wooden floors, intricately-carved ceilings and wide windows open to the ocean breezes. This became the lovers' trysting-place, Lovina allegedly coming and going through a tunnel that began in her garden nearby and led to the wine cellar of the Governor's house.

The idyll ended in 1811 when Sir Thomas departed, giving a large piece of property to Lovina to remember him by. The house remained, referred to as the "Governor's Mansion," and somehow over the years the name of both the house and Galkissa were transformed into Lavinia House and Mount Lavinia. The beauty of the site also remained, making it one of the standard attractions for tourists.

"In the afternoon, of course," wrote the American novelist Frances Parkinson Keyes in 1926, "we must go to Mt. Lavinia—which, as far as we can see, is not a 'mount' at all—to have tea and see the sunset, but finally coming upon a fine hotel originally built for a Governor's residence, where the terrace commands a splendid view of the ocean. That is the orthodox thing for every 'passenger' (tourist) to do in Colombo."

The same year brought another visitor, Lucian Swift Kirtland, who displayed more enthusiasm: "The perfect hour to drive to Mount Lavinia is just before sunset, so as to have the tumultuous gorgeous colorings of the sky and sea as you sit on the terrace conventionally sipping tea. Not always of course, does the sky perform to its full dramatic possibilities; nevertheless I can remember no other place in the Orient where the sunset is so consistently accommodating. Standing on the Lavinia shore close to the tea-house is the most photographed palm tree in all the world. No one ever came here with a camera who did not see the 'possibilities' of that palm tree against the sea."

After serving as a hospital during World War II, the house reopened its doors as the Mount Lavinia Hotel. Among its early guests were movie stars Vivien Leigh, Kirk Douglas and Gregory Peck, all of whom enjoyed its comfort and privacy while working on films in Sri Lanka. Expansions have produced a current total of 275 rooms, all with private balconies and a sea view, in addition to extensive beach frontage; other amenities include four restaurants, a terrace bar, a night-club, a swimming pool, a shopping arcade and a business center.

"For many people," *Newsweek* magazine wrote in 2000, "the romance of the East is inseparable from the old world charm of its colonial era buildings—and none is more romantic than Colombo's Mount Lavinia Hotel… Connoisseurs of gracious living come for the heart-stoppingly beautiful panorama of the Indian Ocean. But equally potent are the ice-cold beers, gin and tonics and whiskey sodas that slip down so smoothly with the setting of the sun."

Doubtless the romance between the Governor and his para-mour have fuelled the imagination of young lovers everywhere, explaining why the Mount Lavinia Hotel is a popular place for local weddings, as well as a favorite destination for honeymooners from all over the world.

Top: Through large arched windows, diners in the now-airconditioned restaurant can enjoy sweeping vistas of the sea and beach.

Left: The bar, simply furnished but softened by a display of potted palms against the white walls.

Top right: Colonial-style furniture in one of the guest rooms includes cane-bottomed chairs and an old-fashioned dressing table.

Right: Countless notable visitors have slept in canopied, colonial-style beds like this one at the Mount Lavinia. During World War II, it served as a hospital.

Page 90: A doorman resplendent in white uniform waits to welcome guests.

Page 91: Façade of the Mount Lavinia, originally built by an early Governor of Ceylon (Sri Lanka) in the early 19th century and later converted into a hotel. Located on a headland just outside Colombo, it still enjoys a reputation as one of the most popular places to view the sun set over the sea.

Clockwise from opposite top left: *The geometric framework of the ceiling light is one of several pleasing architectural touches that can be found throughout the hotel; What can be more inspiring than oceanfront dining? A crow perches momentarily on one of the lamp posts that line the imposing outdoor and west-facing terrace—one of Colombo's favourite sunset spots; A delightful surprise awaits those who explore hidden corners of the hotels. Here a huge Mediterranean inspired Terrace stands largely neglected although it offers magnificent views of the ocean.*

Top: *The front entrance to Mount Lavinia Hotel where guests are met with a fountain and stark white colonial architecture at its best.*

Right: *This art deco inspired balcony and lined windows help to give away the age of this gracious old lady.*

AMANGALLA
GALLE, SRI LANKA
ESTABLISHED 1715

The Aman group has become internationally known for its imaginative, boutique-style hotels in romantic locations that range from the purely sybaritic (Bali, Tahiti and the Thai island of Phuket) to the spectacular (Angkor Wat in Cambodia and Borobudur in Java). One of its newest properties—and one of its most striking—is the Amangalla, within the walls of the old fort at Galle in Sri Lanka.

Near the southern tip of Sri Lanka, Galle has a history that goes back at least a thousand years and perhaps even further, into the mists of legend. Some historians believe Galle was actually the Tarshish of Biblical times, from which King Solomon obtained gems, spices and peacocks. Marco Polo claimed to have stopped there in 1299. Certainly for countless years it was a major port of call for Chinese, Persian, Arab, Indian, and later still, Javanese and Sumatran traders plying the Indian Ocean.

It became known to the Western world in 1505 when a Portuguese fleet bound for the Maldives took refuge from a storm in the harbor. One legend says its name was given when the sailors heard a cock (*galo* in Portuguese) crowing in the town, while another gives the source as the Sinhala word gala (rock); in any case Galle's coat of arms displays a rooster standing on a rock.

Following a dispute with the kingdom of Kandy, the Portuguese established a more permanent presence at Galle, building a Capuchin convent and a small fort of mud and palm leaves called Santa Cruz that was later extended with bastions and walls. When the Dutch captured Galle in 1640, most of these early buildings were destroyed and replaced with far stronger fortifications.

The most impressive of these was the 89-acre (36-hectare) Galle Fort, started in 1663 but not completed until 1715. It had massive bastions and stone ramparts 65 feet (20 meters) thick and numerous buildings lay within its walls, one of which served as headquarters for the Commander. In 1988, the sprawling complex was classified as a World Heritage site by UNESCO.

The Dutch in turn were replaced by the British, who became the first European power to take control of the whole island, then known as Ceylon; in 1802, it became a crown colony and remained one until independence was granted in 1948. Coffee was introduced as the main cash crop during the early 19th century, but when that was destroyed by a blight in the 1870s the plantations—now owned mostly by British

settlers—switched to rubber and, most famously, tea, which thrived in highland areas. By this time Colombo had become the capital and main port. Galle declined in importance, though it remained known for its gemstones and its historic buildings were spared the ravages of later development.

The Fort also remained, its great walls popular as a place to take a pleasant stroll at dusk. "It is the custom of all who do not drive to walk out to ramparts from half-past five to six p.m.," Townsend Harris wrote in his journal in 1855, when he stopped en route to Japan where he became the first American Consul-general. "The views are beautiful and you have a fine fresh air. I always walk here unless occupied by a drive."

Within the walls is a maze of narrow streets and assorted buildings, the older ones dating from the Dutch period, during which an intricate sewer system was also built and flushed out daily by the tide. Among these are a Historical Mansion, a restored Dutch house serving as both a museum of colonial artifacts; a former storehouse that now serves as the National Maritime Museum; the National Museum; and the Dutch Reformed Church, paved with gravestones from the old Dutch cemetery. One group of buildings, first used as headquarters by the Dutch commander and his officers and later as a billet for British soldiers, was combined in 1865 to create the New Oriental Hotel—one of twelve hotels in the Fort at the time—which continued to operate under that name for the next 140 years.

After extensive renovations, these buildings became the Amangalla, the name of which derives from aman ("peace" in Sanskrit) and *galla*, the Sinhalese name for Galle. Four categories of accommodation were created. Seven bedrooms, on the ground level of the Middle Street wing, overlook either the garden or the historic Goote Kerk (Great Church). Six chambers, each with a bedroom and separate sitting area, are located within the Church Street Wing and face the Fort ramparts. Eight suites, six in the Church Street Wing and two in the

Middle Street Wing feature the original polished teak floor-boards and are furnished with both antiques and skilled reproductions. Finally, the Garden House is a two-story structure with a private terrace, a balcony with leafy, treetop views and its own personal butler. There are also two dining rooms, one known in Dutch times as the Zaal (Great Hall) for light meals and afternoon tea and a more formal restaurant that provides a grand setting for dining with a colonial accent. Other facilities include a health spa, a swimming pool and a library.

A step out the front door of these luxurious quarters takes a visitor into the living history of the Fort with its bustling food vendors, bullock carts and Dutch houses with pillared verandahs. Outside the ramparts, the heights of which are still a favored place for late afternoon promenades and socializing, lies Galle itself and a host of other discoveries best explored by foot or bicycle.

The Amangalla opened only a few days before the disastrous tsunami of December 2004 but was spared damage by its thick walls, erected by the Dutch nearly four centuries ago to protect them from a different kind of threat.

Top: Guests can experience the sense of being a part of living history in areas like this, with simple but elegant colonial-style furniture, polished teakwood floors and high, arched windows.

Top right: Guest rooms are furnished with four-poster colonial-style beds that look out on cool, green terraces.

Far right: A sarong-clad attendant opens the white shutters to this glorious bathroom in the Garden Wing. A huge white tub lends even more appeal to this charming bathing space.

Right: The standing lamps—another touch of Aman whimsy—helps re-create a period while at the same time remaining ultra modern.

Page 96: A small round table looks out to the front of the hotel and the delights of Galle Fort beyond. Each of the rooms in the old wing have deep metal shutters which have replaced the more romantic older wooden ones which existed pre-renovation.

Page 97: Thick white walls and a mood of stark simplicity are predominant in the Amangalla, part of a Dutch fort in Galle that was built between 1663 and 1715. It was transformed into a luxury boutique hotel by the Aman group.

Top left: A tall stone wall and coconut palms give both privacy and a tropical atmosphere to the Amangalla's swimming pool.

Left: Private rooms overlook a pool in the hotel's spa, one of the facilities added for the convenience of contemporary guests.

Top: Classic entrance to the hotel; outside it, the busy life of the old fort continues as it has for centuries.

Right: A colonial planter's chair was a characteristic feature of colonial Dutch décor—not surprisingly, as they were built for comfort on those long hot afternoons. White wooden shutters open in the morning and close at night in the extremely attractive rooms of the Garden Wing.

TAPROBANE
WELIGAMA BAY, SRI LANKA
ESTABLISHED 1925

Taprobane is a small, rocky island, covering only a few acres, that rises some fifty yards off the coast of southern Sri Lanka. One of its several owners, the American author Paul Bowles, received a tart response from his wife Jane, also a writer, when he informed her he had bought it in 1950.

Asked by her how one got there, he wrote in a later account, "I explained that you took a ship through the Mediterranean and the Red Sea, crossed part of the Indian Ocean, landed at Colombo and hopped a train which let you off at the fishing village of Weligama. 'And once you're on the island there's nothing between you and the South Pole,' I added. She looked at me for a long moment. 'You'll never get me there,' she said."

The alluring object of Bowles' desire was the creation of an eccentric European aristocrat named Count Maurice Maria de Mauny-Talvande (the title was borrowed from his mother's side of the family). Born in France in 1866, he married the daughter of the British Earl of Strafford in 1898 and had two children. He first came to Sri Lanka, then known as Ceylon, in 1912, staying in the hills as a guest of Sir Thomas Lipton, the tea magnate. The tropical luxuriance was a revelation to him and after some sort of personal crisis in Europe, possibly due to marital and financial problems, he returned in the early 1920s, this time in search of what he described as "one spot which, by its sublime beauty, would fulfill my dreams and hold me there for life."

The quest took several years before he first caught sight of the little island. He swam across the narrow stretch of water and climbed to the top, where, he wrote, "I sat for a long time on a boulder overhanging the sea, wishing that this island lost in the Indian Ocean were mine; picturing and planning what I should do with it. I felt my heart beating with the overwhelming desire to create, the pride of creation, and to find in it peace, the nearest thing to happiness. Yes, it would, it must be, the home which I had dreamt of so many years past."

In due course his dream was realized. (Records show that the island was purchased in 1925, though not in the count's name but rather in that of his son Victor, who was then living in Colombo.) He changed the name from Galduwa, Sinhalese for "rocky island," to the more poetic Taprobane, the old Greek name for Ceylon, and proceeded to build an extraordinary

house. It was octagonal and virtually without walls, covering 135 square feet (12 square meters), with views of the sea and the spectacular garden he planted from almost any point. The result, Bowles observed with approval, "is very rational and, like most things born of fanaticism, wildly impractical."

Here the count took up residence, occasionally entertaining distinguished visitors like the Duchess of Sutherland, to whom a book he wrote in 1937 is dedicated, but concentrating mainly on his garden of exotic specimens gathered from all over the tropical world. He also designed gardens and even furniture, produced by a company he set up in Colombo.

The outbreak of war may have forced him to leave Taprobane; in any event he died of a heart attack in 1941 in the northern city of Jaffna and the island was sold at public auction the following year. Its spell remained potent, however. Bowles lived there in six-month stretches for five years before he was obliged to give it up for personal reasons, selling it to an Irish writer named Shaun Mandy in 1956. Robin Maugham, Somerset's novelist nephew, seriously considered buying it in the early 1970s when he too was looking for "a place of contentment" but regretfully decided that he lacked the "particular cast of character" for such a solitary life. For several years during the 1960s it was owned by the de Silva family, whose most distinguished member was Desmond de Silva, QC, a British barrister. It was later acquired on a long lease by Geoffrey Dobbs, a prominent businessman from Hong Kong, who made the alterations seen today.

The basic form of the house, with its lofty central hall, has been preserved, though its five bedrooms with en suite bathrooms have more privacy than they did in De Mauny's time. A blue infinity-edge pool was also added by the present owner.

The pool, landing and entrance gate were damaged during the tsunami that struck on 26 December 2004—they have now been repaired—but the rest of Taprobane was untouched and remains the dreamlike fantasy that has captured the imaginations of so many for decades.

Left: *Furniture made by local artisans adorn this corner verandah of the house, while white-painted matchstick blinds screen it from the bright tropical sunlight.*

Right: *Supported by slender columns, the original house was octagonal in shape and virtually without walls to allow for maximum flow of air.*

Bottom: *The ocean and tropical garden can be viewed from almost every part of the house. The Count de Mauny-Talvande was particularly proud of the garden; he sourced many of the plant samples himself.*

Page 102: *A portrait of Geoffrey Dobbs, the current owner of Taprobane, sits at the entrance lobby. Surrounded by his memorabilia it adds a personal touch and a glimpse into the very private life of this owner.*

Page 103: *From an infinity pool, one of the later additions to Taprobane by its current owner, only a short stretch of sea separates it from the mainland village of Weligama on the southern coast of Sri Lanka.*

Left: A painting of Taprobane as it looked in the 1930s hangs above a locally-made desk. Note the period rotary-dial telephone and the vase of red gingers gathered from the garden.

Top: A concrete step, a candelabra, red cushions and a wicker planters chair epitomize the lazy comfort that Taprobane offers.

Top right: One of the five bedrooms that the current owner has created, with cool white curtains and a distinctive bedhead decorated with a butterfly.

Right: A four-poster bed, curtained by mosquito netting, offers a view of sea through the door and windows. Each of the five bedrooms in Taprobane is decorated with colonial-style furniture.

Bottom: The blue-tiled infinity pool, built on one of the lower levels of Taprobane, was a recent addition to the house. Offering stunning views of the Indian Ocean, it is a popular spot for guests to relax.

Clockwise from opposite top left: A four-poster bed, curtained by mosquito netting, offers a view of sea through the door and windows. Each of the five bedrooms in Taprobane is decorated with colonial-style furniture; A set of quirky paintings, a red lamp and an old writing desk make a delightful corner in the main living area. Such delightful decorative touches give the house its unique identity; A pathway along the sea leads around one side of the house. The owner has managed to give guest rooms with more privacy than in the original structure while still retaining the unique spirit of the house.

Top: A rustic bench, a coconut palm and an endless panorama of sea and sky epitomize the sense of peace and solitude that the founder of Taprobane sought. When the coast of Sri Lanka was hit by a tsunami in December 2004, the house only sustained light damage.

GRAND HOTEL
NUWARA ELIYA, SRI LANKA
ESTABLISHED 1826

Located at an altitude of over 6,000 feet (1,830 meters), Nuwara Eliya has a cool, crisp climate (the mean annual temperature is 59 degrees Fahrenheit/15 degrees Celsius), clear mountain streams and impressive views of the surrounding countryside. It was thus not surprising that early in their occupation of Sri Lanka, or Ceylon as it was known then, the British found it eminently suitable for one of the hill-stations that they established throughout most of their tropical empire. As elsewhere, they set about creating a nostalgic facsimile of home, with mock-Tudor bungalows, rose gardens, open fireplaces, an Anglican church, a lake for boating and fishing, and trails for walking in the brisk, invigorating air, so different from the humid heat of Colombo on the sea far below.

Quarters for convalescent soldiers were established in 1828 at Nuwara Eliya, which also became an agricultural station in an unsuccessful attempt to acclimatize the Andean cinchona tree (the source of quinine). Around the same time (the exact date seems uncertain; one source says it was 1826) Sir Edward Barnes, who served as Governor General of the island, built a summer residence for himself; and after considerable alterations and additions this became the three-story Grand Hotel, the preferred place to stay for visitors who did not have a house of their own.

The heyday of the Grand (and Nuwara Eliya generally) was during the 1920s and '30s. During the summer months it was crowded with homesick Englishmen and their memsahibs, who enjoyed golf at the meticulously tended 18-hole course across from the hotel, strolls through aromatic forests of conifers, a bit of game hunting (though the last elephant was shot in 1930), and perhaps a discreet love affair or two. There was also a botanical garden where the agricultural station once stood, planted now with temperate ornamentals like roses and rhododendrons instead of cinchona trees. The church boasted a stained-glass window donated by Queen Victoria (another was given later by Queen Elizabeth II). There was also the exclusive Hill Club, founded in 1876, which admitted no locals or women until 1967, long after most of the English had departed.

The hills below were terraced into vast estates for growing tea, Sri Lanka's most famous product. These remain today, all along the winding road that leads up to Nuwara Eliya. They form a neat carpet of green that covers the mountains, enlivened by Tamil women in colorful saris who move through the shrubs deftly picking tender leaves and buds.

The Grand Hotel, now under the management of the Tangerine Group, also remains, only slightly altered from British days. An avenue of lofty fir trees lines the drive to the entrance, the public lounges are furnished with heavy wooden chairs near the warmth of open fireplaces and a huge chandelier illuminates the main restaurant, which still offers such fare as roast beef and Yorkshire pudding. Passageways lead to 156 guest rooms and suites in two main wings, the Governor's Wing and the Golf Wing, with views of either a neat garden or the Nuwara Eliya golf course. There are three well-stocked bars, a games room with three billiard tables, a supper club with nightly music, and a more recent addition, an Indian restaurant with outside seating during the day and a counter for take-away food.

The coolest months of the year in Nuwara Eliya are January and February, when sweaters and jackets are welcome and on a misty or rainy day the nostalgic memories of life "back home" must surely have been particularly acute to expatriate guests.

By far the most popular month these days though, is April. Not only are the temperatures at their highest in the lowlands at this time, but it also coincides with the Sinhalese and Tamil New Year festivities, which means a significant influx of visitors from all over Sri Lanka. They spend their time watching horse races, going on scenic treks up nearby Mount Pidurutalaga, the island's highest mountain, or visiting popular attractions like Hakgala Gardens, which was once a cinchona plantation and is now famous for its flourishing roses.

Though the clientele may have changed over the years, the Grand and the quaint little town around it still preserve the "bit of England" atmosphere that so entranced visitors of the past.

Clockwise from far left: *Chandeliers cast a warm glow over the entrance hallway of the hotel. The hotel is especially popular during winter months as it offers a welcome respite from the heat of the lowlands; The Main Restaurant uses Victorian furniture and decor to create a colonial atmosphere; Beige lounge chairs and filtered sunlight make for a very cosy corner even during the chilliest Nuwara Eliya afternoons; Sitting areas with polished teak floors, period chairs and tall windows look out towards the gardens that surround the hotel.*

Right: *A guest room, decorated in pale, soothing colors and with a bowl of freshly cut roses from the garden. The hotel has 156 guest rooms, including 3 presidential suites.*

Bottom right: *The white bathroom decor, highlighted by a vase of soft yellow flowers, makes for a very classic—but still refreshing—look for the bathrooms.*

Page 110: *The hotel garden has shaded tables and chairs so guests can enjoy the refreshing outdoor air*

Page 111: *The entrance to the Grand Hotel in Nuwara Eliya, a former agricultural station which became a popular hot-season retreat for British residents during the colonial period. It boasts temperate-zone ornamental plants that thrive at the higher altitude.*

THE STRAND
YANGON, MYANMAR
ESTABLISHED 1901

Built by a British entrepreneur named John Darwood at the beginning of the 20th century, the Strand was acquired by Aviet Sarkies, one of the famous Armenian brothers who already had prestigious hotels in Penang and Singapore. Aviet, said to be the most retiring of the brothers, had opened a modest hostelry in Rangoon called the Sarkies Hotel. With the Strand, however, which opened in 1901, he embarked on a much more ambitious venture and turned it into one of the Burmese capital's most noted landmarks.

The elegant three-story colonial-style structure, overlooking the bustling waterfront, was in the heart of Rangoon's business district and thus convenient for both local residents and visitors arriving by ship. The 1911 edition of Murray's classic *Handbook for Travellers in India, Burma, and Ceylon* described it as being "patronized by royalty, nobility and distinguished personages," and it was Burma's best-known hotel for many years thereafter. (One noted literary traveler who did not stay there, however, was Somerset Maugham, with whom so many historic Asian hotels proudly claim an association. In his account of a trip to Burma, Siam and Indo-China, *The Gentleman in the Parlour,* he does not mention the Strand or exactly where he stayed while in the city, only that it was "a spacious, shady house in a garden.")

Twice, in the 1920s and then again in the '30s, the Strand's interior was gutted by fires (perhaps that was why Maugham stayed elsewhere), but each time it was restored and expanded. However it experienced more serious and lasting damage during World War II, when Rangoon was captured and occupied by the Japanese for four years.

After Burma achieved independence in 1948, the Strand enjoyed a brief revival under the management of London's Steel Brothers Company. The property was nationalized in 1963 by the government of General Ne Win and then, like so many other reminders of Rangoon's colonial heritage began a slow but relentless decline into shabbiness as the country embarked on the economically disastrous Burmese Road to Socialism.

Memories of the Strand, a publication issued by the present owners, manages to find some amusement in this otherwise gloomy 26-year period: "You could imagine the Strand then as a beautiful lady in faded glory, but with a glimmer of humor in her eyes as she peered down at her hem where mice scrabbled. Oh yes, there were mice, but they were not any other mice, they were the STRAND mice. They were of all sizes and colors ranging from glistening black to peachy beige; they were not scraggly, dusty furred creatures. In fact, they looked very well turned out, clean and frisky with happy whiskers and bright eyes. They could be seen scampering on the stage behind bridal couples, peering from behind the bar, and on the rare occasions when there was a concert in the hall, jumping under the legs of the piano in time to the speed of the music."

The few tourists who came during those days are apt to recall the "mice" as being old-fashioned rats. But still many visitors still preferred to stay in the decaying old structure rather than at one of the characterless official hotels offered as an alternative. "Shut your mind to [the] minor drawbacks," advised the Lonely Planet guidebook in 1979, "and enjoy the Strand's other advantages—its conveniently central location, its pleasant bar and lounge area, its excellent and remarkably economical restaurant, and all-round cheerful service."

Change came at last in 1991 when a company headed by the entrepreneur Adrian Zecha, better known as the founder of the celebrated Amanresorts, began a renovation project that would cost more than $12 million. The Strand reopened in late 1993 and by early 1995 it was offering 32 suites, equipped with the latest in modern comforts, beautifully furnished with local art and antiques and serviced by a team of butlers day and night. Renovation of a once-popular annexe was planned but abandoned in 1998 for economic reasons.

Now operated by General Hotel Management, the Strand also has a café with tall windows looking out onto Strand Road, a grill room with a vaulted ceiling and gold-and-black lacquer paintings from Burma's ancient capital of Bagan (Pagan), a bar and a ballroom that holds up to a thousand people for receptions. All these public facilities were utilized in 2001 when the Strand celebrated its centennial with a series of festive events.

Top: The carved wooden entrance to the Strand Grill; the gold-and-black lacquer paintings on the far wall came from the ancient capital of Bagan, still famous for its artisans in this medium.

Far left: The upper floor of the Strand, with carved teak banisters and a skylight with art deco decorations.

Left: A guest suite in the hotel; the old structure was completely renovated in the early 1990s, though great pains were taken to retain its old-world charm

Right: A bartender mixes a drink in The Strand Bar, which is still a popular gathering place in the late afternoons.

Bottom: The Strand Suite features a master bedroom, study, living room and dining room with attached pantry. Here, glass-panelled doors and fan skylights evoke some of the best of British colonial architecture.

Page 114: An attendant at the Strand wearing a longgi, or traditional Burmese sarong.

Page 115: Entrance to the Strand, which opened in 1901. It was one of several legendary Asian hotels founded by the Armenian Sarkies brothers; others that still remain are the Eastern and Oriental in Penang and Raffles Hotel in Singapore.

Clockwise from opposite left: Antiques such as this old Burmese jar converted into a lamp, are displayed throughout the Strand; A corner detail of the bar where potted palms are almost mandatory and slatted cane blinds add the right touch; A napkin folded into the shape of a lotus blossom serves as a table decoration in the restaurant; The massive columns outside The Strand give the hotel its unique façade. The large glazed jars between each column are made by local artisans.

Right: The Strand Bar, which overlooks the busy street outside, serves up a full mix of cocktails for thirsy guests.

Bottom: The Strand, like most of Asia's historic hotels, is located just a short walk from the river port where visitors arrived in the old days, when boats were the main form of transportation to far-flung destinations.

THE ORIENTAL
BANGKOK, THAILAND
ESTABLISHED 1884

In 1976, when it opened a lofty new River Wing, the Oriental announced that it was celebrating its 100th birthday. Actually, the date was somewhat arbitrary; at least two establishments bearing that name had existed near the same site as far back as 1865, when one of them is recorded as being burned in a great fire. Another was in operation by 1878, operated by two Danish seamen and offering "family accommodations," perhaps to distinguish it from the other rather rowdy guesthouses that were then the only places where visitors to the Thai capital might find a room.

The Oriental hotel of today originated in 1884 when the property was acquired by H.N. Andersen, a Dane who had prospered from shipping (he would eventually found the huge East Asiatic Company) and who felt the time was ripe for Bangkok to have a hotel that would equal those then rising in ports like Singapore and Rangoon.

He filled in a swampy plot of land on the Chao Phraya River, just a short distance from New Road, Bangkok's first proper street, and hired a local firm of Italian architects to design an imposing structure that opened three years later. "It has forty commodious and well-furnished rooms," reported the *Bangkok Times*. "We have been asked to say that no invitations have been sent out for the opening... but the proprietors Messrs Andersen & Co. wish all to know they will be welcome on that occasion from 4 p.m. onwards when the fountains of magnanimity will be turned on and rain hospitality all round."

Almost all of Bangkok's foreign community and aristocratic Thais came to see the new wonder. Most guests arrived by boat and some by carriage, and all were duly impressed. The hotel consisted of two wings at the time, each two stories high, and a central section crowned by a pediment displaying a golden rising sun. Within were carpets from Brussels, a talented barman named Spider, divans covered in peacock-blue velvet, mahogany furniture and a chef named Georges Troisouefs who had once worked for the French legation.

The Oriental soon became the place to stay for visiting dignitaries and the favored social center for local residents. King Chulalongkorn came for a personal inspection in 1890, and officers in the entourage of the future Czar Nicholas II of Russia were offered free hospitality the following year.

The Oriental's fortunes rose and fell over the next 50-odd years. Andersen sold it to Louis T. Leonowens, son of Anna of *The King and I* fame, after which it changed hands frequently. Somerset Maugham almost died there in early 1923, from a fever contracted in northern Burma, and in his delirium overheard the German manageress tell the doctor to get him out before the end came. During World War II, the hotel was occupied by the Japanese and operated by the Imperial Hotel of Tokyo; afterwards it housed liberated Allied prisoners of war and declined into increasing shabbiness, stripped of almost all its furnishings.

Up for sale yet again, the Oriental was acquired by a group of investors that included Jim Thompson, an architect by training, who planned to restore the structure to its former glory for the tourists who were beginning to trickle back into Thailand. Thompson left the group to start the Thai silk industry that would later make him famous, but under a French manageress and former journalist named Germaine Krull, the Oriental slowly started to recover.

The hotel's Bamboo Bar was opened and quickly became a popular gathering place. In 1958, the 10-story Tower Wing was erected, boasting Bangkok's first elevator and a French restaurant, Le Normandie, on the upper floor. The Oriental changed ownership again in 1967, when a local company called Italthai, which merged with the Mandarin Hotel group in 1972, bought it. That same year an adjacent piece of property was acquired between the hotel and the French Embassy, on which the 350-room River Wing was built in 1973.

The only part of the Oriental today that dates from the original structure is the atmospheric Author's Wing. It offers afternoon tea on the ground floor and above, suites named after Joseph Conrad, Somerset Maugham, Noel Coward and James Michener. (While there is some doubt as to whether Conrad ever stayed at the hotel—he was a poor seaman when he came to Bangkok in 1888—the others certainly did.)

The Oriental was first named the best hotel in the world in 1976 by an American magazine for bankers; since then, it has been honored in countless lists and continues to reign supreme as a Bangkok social center despite numerous competitors.

Left: A screen with figures from traditional northern Thai mural paintings forms part of the decorations in the luxurious spa opened by the Oriental across the river from its main buildings.

Bottom left: The Thai silk used in the upholstery adds to the sense of richness in the sitting area of a guest suite. A painting in traditional Thai style hangs over the sofa, while a Laotian rain drum serves as a side table on the far right.

Right: A carved wooden figure of a mythological bird is one of the decorative items in an old building across the river that houses the Oriental's Thai cooking school.

Page 120: All-white wicker furniture with green-patterned cushions create a restful atmosphere in the lower lobby of the Oriental's Author's Wing, where afternoon tea is served daily.

Page 121: Exterior of the Author's Wing, overlooking the garden on the bank of the Chao Phraya River. Suites in this wing, the oldest part of the Oriental, are named after Somerset Maugham, Joseph Conrad, Noel Coward and other famous writers who have stayed at the hotel over its long history.

Far left: Paneled teak walls and polished floors contribute to the serenity of a treatment room in the spa, one of the first opened by a hotel in Thailand.

Left: A corner of the entrance to the Oriental's award-winning spa. Made in an old Thai timber house, the spa features herbal steam baths and private treatment rooms with attached shower facilities.

Top: A shuttle boat with a characteristic multi-level Thai roof plies the Chao Phraya River, carrying guests to and from the hotel and its Thai restaurant, cooking school and spa. The façade of the restaurant, seen on the far bank, was originally part of an old temple.

Left: Old ceramic tiles in a floral pattern add a touch of period charm; the attendant crossing them is in traditional Thai costume.

Clockwise from top right: Ornately carved wooden vents over doors and windows were widely used throughout the original Oriental to increase air circulation; A graceful double staircase leads up to suites on the second floor of the Author's Wing—a feathery stand of bamboo on the left contributes a touch of green to the airy lightness; The lobby of the Author's Wing, where afternoon tea is served; Exterior of the Author's Wing in the evening, facing the river and originally the entrance to the hotel. The garden is densely planted with traveler's palms and other tropical ornamentals to create a jungle-like effect.

THE SOFITEL
RAILWAY HOTEL
HUA HIN, THAILAND
ESTABLISHED 1923

In 1913, a Thai prince and his Russian wife built a bungalow on the beach at Hua Hin, on the west coast of the Gulf of Thailand, and may thus be credited with starting the long association between Bangkok's aristocracy and the sleepy fishing village. The opening of the southern railway line in the 1920s made travel easier from the capital and soon other families were building summer homes at Hua Hin, among them the King, whose palace there, completed in 1929, was called Klai Klangwan or "Far From Care."

A Thai prince and his Russian wife made the then difficult journey from Bangkok to Hua Hin, a small fishing village on the west coast of the Gulf of Thailand, in 1913. They were so entranced by the clean, sandy beach and the cool sea breezes that they were inspired to build a bungalow there, and may be credited with starting the association between Thai aristocrats and what is now a popular resort.

The opening of Thailand's southern railway line in the early 1920s made travel from the capital to Hua Hin much easier and soon other prominent families built summer homes there. Most notable of Hua Hin's new residents was the King of Thailand. His palace, completed in 1929, was called Klai Klangwan, "Far From Care." (Ironically, he was staying here when he received word of the coup d'etat that ended the country's absolute monarchy in 1932.)

Because of such eminent visitors, the State Railways of Thailand, which had a string of simple rest houses along its various routes, decided it had to offer something considerably more impressive for Hua Hin. The result, opened in 1923, was a splendid Edwardian fantasy built mostly of teakwood, offering large breezy rooms with high ceilings and broad verandahs overlooking the sea. The German-born wife of another Thai prince was the first housekeeper, and an English gardener was hired to create a fanciful topiary landscape which included a larger-than-life-sized elephant that spanned a walkway. Not far away was an excellent golf course, one of the first in Thailand, described in a 1929 guidebook as "second to none east of Suez."

After the events of 1932, which led to the temporary exile of a number of its royal residents, Hua Hin's prestige suffered a gradual decline. This accelerated after World War II with the rise

of much livelier tourist facilities at Pattaya, on the opposite side of the Gulf, closer to Bangkok by road and easier to reach. The Railway Hotel, too, in spite of its gracious proportions, became seedier. In 1970, a notorious serial killer named Charles Sobhraj attempted to poison two victims in one of its suites; they were saved only by the timely intervention of a staff member who found them unconscious and summoned help.

In the 1980s, a new generation discovered the charms of Hua Hin, some of them younger members of the old families. Hotels and condominiums rose along the beach and the royal family began spending a good deal of their time at Klai Klangwan. The King initiated several of his experimental agricultural projects nearby.

The Railway Hotel, by then acquired by the Central Group of Bangkok, was in need of a major overhaul. It was scheduled for demolition when, by chance, the producers of *The Killing Fields* used it to portray a hotel in Phnom Penh for their film about Cambodia's civil war. The owners were so beguiled by its unexpected beauty that they determined to preserve it and add other facilities on the property to meet more modern needs.

These include 177 rooms and 30 suites, three swimming pools, and a spa offering many treatments. A museum displays artifacts from the old days, while the Elephant Bar has a pianist and a collection of antiques. In the Railway Wing, the original rooms with high ceilings, verandahs and polished teak floors retain all their old appeal, especially for visitors with a taste for nostalgia.

Now under the management of the Sofitel group, the old Railway and its meticulously-maintained topiary garden constitute a soothing reminder of what Hua Hin was like over eighty years ago when it became Thailand's first seaside resort.

Clockwise from top left: Sunlight and shadows create an interesting afternon detail on one of the walls of the original part of the hotel; Wooden slatted details characterize the round pavilion that houses the hotel's top colonial suites; A grand imposing staircase curves its way down to the main open air lobby—a symphony of polished white tiles and broad vistas that look out to the wide lawns and beyond to the sea; The entrance lobby with black-and-white marble tiles, colonial-style furniture and a view of the hotel's famous topiary garden outside. This area was carefully restored when the Railway Hotel was expanded. Special attention was paid to retaining its original open-air atmosphere.

Top: A curving staircase and a palm—stunning architectural subtleties such as this make the hotel a delight to explore.

Page 126: The old wing of the Railway Hotel dates back to 1923. This open structure of white verandahs and red-tiled roofs looks out onto the beach of Hua Hin.

Page 127: A verandah on the upper level of the old wing; comfortable teakwood lounge chairs offer views of the garden.

129

Right: Guest room in the hotel's older section, with simple teak-wood furniture and tall windows offering a panoramic view of the sea. The hotel has 207 rooms, 30 of which are suites.

Bottom: The stunning swimming pool looks out to the Gulf of Thailand and was added during the hotel's extensive renovation in the 1980s.

Top: The entrance to the Railway Hotel, a white teakwood structure that first opened in 1923; it was the largest and most impressive of a string of guest accommodations built by the Royal State Railways in the 1920s and 30s.

Left: Pathways allow guests to enjoy pleasant strolls through the lush gardens on the hotel grounds.

Bottom: The Grand Suite in the colonial section of the hotel has a private balcony where guests can take in the scenery.

RAFFLES GRAND HOTEL
D'ANGKOR
SIEM REAP, CAMBODIA
ESTABLISHED 1932

Ever since the French explorer and naturalist Henri Mouhot stumbled on them in 1860, the spectacular ruins of the kingdom of Angkor, lost in the jungle near the Cambodian town of Siem Reap have exerted a powerful spell on travelers. "One looks, one admires, and, seized with respect, one is silent," Mouhot wrote in the journal that first brought Angkor to international attention. "For where are the words to praise a work of art that may not have its equal anywhere on the globe?"

During the colonial era French archaeologists, some of whom spent a lifetime on the project, painstakingly restored not only the great Angkor Wat, the world's largest religious complex, but also many of the other temples and monuments in the vicinity. Tourists began to come too, although not in very large numbers because of the physical difficulties of reaching Siem Reap (it took Somerset Maugham four days to get there from Bangkok in 1923, by tramp steamer, car, and finally by sampan across the great Tonle Sap lake). Still, there were enough visitors to justify some sort of accommodations within easy distance of the ruins.

Several modest guest houses opened, one directly across the causeway leading to Angkor Wat, but the first really imposing facility was the Grand Hotel D'Angkor, some five miles (eight kilometers) from the temples. It began operations toward the end of 1932 and for the next 40 years was the preferred place to stay for those who wanted to see the famous ruins in style and comfort. King Noradom Sihanouk brought Jacqueline Kennedy there in 1967, when she came on a private visit with David Ormsby-Gore, and staged a performance of classical dance by moonlight on the vast terrace of Angkor Wat.

Cambodia's civil war engulfed the country in the early 1970s, eventually driving out both archaeologists and casual visitors. When the murderous Khmer Rouge took control in 1975, Siem Reap, like most other cities and towns, was largely emptied of its population (the bones of many are preserved in a local Buddhist temple as a grim monument to this terrible period), though the ruins themselves remained untouched. So, remarkably, was the Grand Hotel, and when tourists started arriving at the beginning of the 1990s it was there to welcome them. Conditions were hardly luxurious however. One guest of the period recalls erratic supplies of water and electricity, dingy furnishings and armies of rats that patrolled the halls by night.

Rescue came when Singapore-based Raffles International took over the hotel and embarked on a large-scale job of restoration and redevelopment that was completed in December 1997. The four-story main building was preserved, but was refurbished with taste and imagination. Period antiques are casually displayed, an old-fashioned cage elevator rises to upper floors and vintage photographs and posters create a nostalgic ambiance. One of the latter is by George Groslier, a French artist who started the School of Cambodian Arts in Phnom Penh in the 1930s to train artisans in the old Khmer decorative techniques. Central air-conditioning, cable television and modern bathrooms, were also installed (with a private generator to ensure everything works even when Siem Reap experiences one of its occasional power failures).

Two low-rise wings in the same colonial style were added at the rear on either side, bringing the total number of rooms up to 131. Between the new wings is a spectacular 115-foot (35-meter) swimming pool, Siem Reap's first at the time. There are also five restaurants, a basement bar fancifully decorated with elephant motifs and a fully-equipped spa offering massages and other health treatments.

The hotel is justly proud of the 14-acre (5.6-hectare) park it has restored in an area between the front entrance and a summer palace belonging to the royal family. Some 20,000 trees, palms and flowering shrubs grow here along walkways that can be enjoyed by the public as well as by guests on afternoon strolls.

There are now direct flights daily to Siem Reap from Bangkok and other points and many of the 1.7 million tourists who came to Cambodia in 2006 want to see Angkor. Major new international hotels are rising as a consequence, as well as a host of smaller facilities; but the Grand maintains its dowager-like prominence in the midst of all this activity, a reminder of what travel was like in the old days.

Top left: *Local furniture, textiles and handicrafts are used to decorate the hotel's main lobby. Built on a 15-acre (six-hectare) site, the hotel is located just five miles (eight kilometers) from the famous temples of Angkor.*

Left: *Marble tiles in a pattern of black and white and an old engraving of the Angkor temples adorn this hallway leading to the guest rooms. The hotel has 131 rooms decorated with country-style furniture and locally-produced pieces.*

Top: *View of the lobby, furnished with reproductions of old benches; a Hindu sculpture stands on the table in the background.*

Right: *An antique cabinet and teakwood bed behind one of the Grand's original railings. To help capture the original atmosphere of the hotel, some of the original fittings were salvaged and refurbished during the hotel's renovation.*

Page 132: *A writing desk and Tiffany lamp define a cosy corner in one of the elegant rooms of the Grand Hotel D'Angkor.*

Page 133: *A large swimming pool was added to the Grand Hotel during its extensive renovation by the Raffles group in the late 1990s. A pair of enormous stone Khmer-style lions serve as water spouts, while the domed building behind is in ancient Cambodian style.*

135

Clockwise from top left: The hotel's Landmark Rooms feature beds with hand-carved wooden posts. The rooms are decorated with a mix of locally-produced and art deco pieces that reflect the hotel's unique history; Great pains were taken to blend Cambodian and art deco pieces into the hotel's decor when it was being restored; The mix of art deco and locally-made items is effectively used to preserve the Grand Hotel D'Angkor's unique historical and architectural heritage.

Top: Opened in 1932, the Grand Hotel D'Angkor survived years of neglect and the violence of Khmer Rouge rule before it was taken over and restored by the Raffles group. This view shows the back of the three-story building, overlooking the swimming pool.

Right: Luxurious old-world bathroom fittings pamper guests and stay true to the Grand Hotel D'Angkor's long history.

Raffles Hotel
Le Royal
PHNOM PENH, CAMBODIA
ESTABLISHED 1929

Though something of a backwater in the days of French Indo-China, the Cambodian capital of Phnom Penh nevertheless had a distinctive charm that captivated many visitors, colonial and otherwise. Somerset Maugham, however, was not among its admirers when he came in 1923. Eager to be on his way to the fabled glories of Angkor Wat, he stayed only a few days and merely noted its "broad streets with arcades in which there are Chinese shops, formal gardens and, facing the river, a quay neatly planted with trees like the quay in a French riverside town. The hotel is large, dirty and pretentious, and there is a terrace outside it where the merchants and functionaries may take an aperitif and for a moment forget they are not in France."

If he had come a few years later, Maugham might have taken a more benign view. Le Royal, a hotel in a grander style than the one where he stayed, opened in 1929 and would certainly have appealed to this inveterate traveler. And if he had lingered longer, he probably would have been seduced by the leisurely pace of life in the little city (at the time it had a population of only around 25,000) with its pedicabs, its profusion of tropical growth, its French restaurants and its friendly, smiling people.

It remained that way for a remarkably long time, despite upheavals in neighboring countries, throughout World War II and even the early 1970s, when catastrophe was only a few hundred kilometers beyond the city limits. Le Royal, boasting a handsome colonial façade and art deco interior, impeccable service and superb cuisine, was the center of local social life, as well as the place where most visitors stayed, usually on their way to and from Angkor. King Noradom Sihanouk often put up official guests there, among them Charles de Gaulle, Andre Malraux, and Jacqueline Kennedy.

It was thus only natural that when foreign journalists began to arrive, Le Royal became the preferred headquarters for most. Jon Swain, a reporter for the Agence France-Presse, flew in to cover the coup d'etat that ousted Sihanouk in 1970. He was driven straight to the hotel and "liked its romantic air at once. Its carved wooden staircase leading to what seemed like miles of dimly lit corridors, the garden lush with strange plants, with a pool at the back, the faded pictures of Angkor on its snuff-colored walls, the machine-gun rattle of French from old rubber planters downing Pernods at the bar."

Swain made his home in Studio Six, a two-bedroom duplex on the ground floor. In *River of Time*, a moving memoir of his Indo-China experiences, he fondly recalls Le Royal as "a place where the foreign community, particularly the French, congregated. Each day saw long-legged French girls grace the pool. Their presence conjured up an irresistible atmosphere of hot sex and ice-cold drinks. La Sirene, the outdoor restaurant, served fresh lobster, crab and a delicious fish called Les Demoiselles du Mekong."

These happy days were to end all too soon. Le Royal changed its name to Le Phnom, in recognition of Cambodia's new status as a republic. Despite massive American military assistance (some have argued that it was because of such assistance), the mysterious rebel force known as the Khmer Rouge steadily moved closer and eventually surrounded the city. Shells rained on once peaceful streets and markets, and more than a million refugees poured into Phnom Penh. "The bombardments were so intense," wrote Swain, "that journalists abandoned their rooms at the top of Le Phnom, which were fully exposed to rocket and artillery. Monsieur Loup, the manager, offered the higher rooms for US$5, but even at that knock-down price he had few takers."

The city fell on 15 April 1975. The journalists and other foreigners took refuge in the French Embassy until they were evacuated by land to Thailand, while the entire local population was forced into the countryside, where they endured a nightmare that lasted four years and cost many of them their lives.

In 1980, after the Vietnamese had driven the Khmer Rouge out, Jon Swain returned to Phnom Penh. The Le Royal was now

renamed the Samaki, or Solidarity, Hotel and was being used by international aid agencies. "It was in a poor state, its garden weed-grown, its pool filled with stagnant water; I looked in something of a daze at the studio where I had lived, now occupied by a Swiss aid worker," he wrote.

The hotel closed in 1993, but happier times lay ahead. A few years later Singapore-based Raffles International took over its operation (as they had also done with the Raffles Grand Hotel d'Angkor in Siem Reap—see page 132), gave it back its original name, and after a complete restoration and expansion costing some US$50 million, reopened its doors in 1997 as a modern facility with 210 guest rooms. These are spread throughout three low-rise wings, one of them the original historic building, all overlooking a garden courtyard and a new swimming pool. Le Royal also has eight restaurants and bars, a business center, and a spa offering relaxing therapeutic treatments. Additions have been designed to fit in as unobtrusively as possible with the colonial design of the old hotel that charmed so many in the past.

Bottom: View of the lobby, where a handsome teakwood table displays an impressive flower arrangement and period lighting fixtures provide a reminder of Le Royal's past.

Clockwise from right: The entrance to the hotel's popular Elephant Bar, which gets its name from the elephant motifs painted on its ceiling. The bar serves a cocktail, Femme Fatale, created in honor of Jacqueline Kennedy; Tall, graceful archways and wide doorways create an atmosphere of lofty coolness in the lobby; Like most hotels of the period, the Le Royal was not originally equipped with air conditioning. The high archways helped air circulate throughout the building.

Page 138: The Le Royal Hotel first opened in 1929. The spreading, fan-like leaves of a traveler's palm can be seen just inside the gate.

Page 139: The dining room of the hotel was lovingly restored by the Raffles group in a renovation that took four years in the early 1990s.

Left: The Restaurant Le Royal serves a selection of French and Cambodian cuisine and is often patronized by Phnom Penh's leading lights. The mirrored archway enhances the already generous proportions of the room.

Bottom: Art deco lamps and the tall archway add interesting visual elements to the simple counter in the hotel lobby.

Clockwise from right: The Le Royal Suite is the hotel's premier suite and features French and Cambodian furnishings; Black and white floor tiles were a common feature of colonial-era hotels, and reflects the Le Royal's origins; Wide and tall archways were essential to allow cool air to flow through the building as the hotel did not have air conditioning when it was first built.

Top: The entrance to the Raffles Amritra Spa; open beams allow a view of the clay tiles covering the walkway, along both sides of which are views of the hotel garden. The spa offers numerous relaxation and rejuvenation treatments and boasts a variety of facilities including an outdoor lap pool, Jacuzzi and a fitness center.

Right: The swimming pool was added to the hotel during its restoration. A huge rain tree spreads its branches in front of the white-columned façade which was a common architectural feature of the time.

SOFITEL
METROPOLE
HANOI, VIETNAM
ESTABLISHED 1901

Of all the cities in what was once known as French Indochina, none was more French in atmosphere and appearance than Hanoi. By the beginning of the 20th century, it had an orderly grid of broad, tree-lined boulevards, elegant public buildings (among them an opera house and the headquarters of the Banque de l'Indochine), and pastel-colored villas set in shady gardens for the officials who ruled this jewel of their Asian possessions. In 1901, these were joined by the Metropole Hotel, built by two private French investors who felt the city needed a suitably impressive place to stay for Hanoi's increasing visitor arrivals.

With its classical façade, louvered shutters, wrought-iron decorations, and carefully tended courtyard lawn, the Metropole fulfilled this function admirably. The guest list ranged from government dignitaries on their regular colonial tours to international figures like Charlie Chaplin and Paulette Goddard (who came on their honeymoon in the 1930s). Somerset Maugham, who found Hanoi too familiar to be of much interest ("the French tell you it is the most attractive town in the East, but when you ask them why, answer that it is exactly like a town, Montpellier or Grenoble, in France"), instead spent most of his time in his room working on *The Gentleman in the Parlour*, his only true travel book, about a journey through Burma, Siam and Indo-China. The hotel also served as a social center for local residents and for special events such as the first movie ever shown in Hanoi.

Nor did World War II have the devastating effect on the Metropole that it did on so many of Asia's other historic hotels. Though they used the colony as a staging post for their invasion of Malaya and the Dutch East Indies, the Japanese left the French more or less in control until almost the end of the war, and the hotel continued to operate as usual.

It also continued operations during the eight-year conflict between the French and the Viet Minh that ended with Vietnam being divided at the 17th parallel and Hanoi coming into the hands of Ho Chi Minh's forces. Bernard Fall, who reported on that war in *Street Without Joy*, described the Metropole as being "the last really fashionable place in Hanoi. Louis Blouet, its manager, exacted high standards of performance from his staff, which was as well-styled as that of his brother's Hotel George V in Paris and whose tipping scale was considerably lower than that of his Paris establishment. The headwaiter—a former colonel in the Chinese Nationalist forces—was as suave as his

Paris counterpart and the barman could produce a reasonable facsimile of almost any civilized drink except water." Graham Greene no doubt enjoyed a fair share of those drinks when not working on his famous Vietnam novel *The Quiet American* in his room at the hotel.

Changes definitely took place, however, when the French left and Hanoi became the capital of the Democratic Republic of Vietnam in 1954. When a new war with the south expanded into a major conflict that brought in the United States and others, the Metropole became the Thong Nhat and its guests were mostly Russian military advisers and eastern Europeans. There were, however, a few American visitors who came by a complex route via Laos to demonstrate their opposition to the war and provide eyewitness accounts of Hanoi's bombing.

Jane Fonda, for example, stayed there on the celebrated trip that earned her the epithet "Hanoi Jane" when she posed beside the wreckage of an American bomber. So did writer and critic Mary McCarthy, who praised the Thong Nhat for offering plenty of hot water, as well as such luxuries as "sheets of toilet paper laid out on a box in a fan pattern (keys at the desk were laid out in a fan pattern, too), a thermos of hot water for making tea, a package of tea, a teapot, cups and saucers, candies, cigarettes and a mosquito net draped over the bed and tucked in."

Though it survived the bombing, the Metropole was definitely showing its age by the time the war finally ended. So, at least, thought Pulitzer-Prize-winning journalist Neil Sheehan when Americans were allowed back and he came with his wife on his first visit to Hanoi in 1986. "When I walked up the front steps of the hotel, past Grecian columns of peeling white paint, and pushed on the revolving door at the entrance, it turned grudgingly," Sheehan wrote. "The explanation was not in the

Top: An outdoor terrace with wrought-iron furniture, with the dining room behind. Called the Thong Nhat during the war years when Hanoi was the capital of North Vietnam, the hotel reverted to its old name in 1992 after a major renovation.

Clockwise from top right: A Vietnamese-style lamp adds an authentic touch to this corner of the hotel lobby; A private booth at the Le Beaulieu restaurant, which is renowned for its French cuisine; The lush greenery of the Metropole's garden creates a tropical paradise in the midddle of downtown Hanoi.

Page 146: The Metropole has stood proudly for over 100 years and has played host to numerous celebrities and dignitaries in that period of time.

Page 147: The façade of the Metropole was designed when Hanoi was the capital of French Indochina and was intended to remind visitors of France. It survived the wars fought by the French and later the Americans and South Vietnamese.

heaviness of the once-handsome door: almost everything in Hanoi has been running down since 1939. The spindle on which the revolving door turned was worn out. Decades of guests coming and going, grinding grit underfoot, had also created dips in the marble of the entrance steps and the floor of the lobby. We went up to a room assigned to us on the third floor. It was large and held two old wooden beds with mosquito netting and a new Japanese refrigerator in an opposite corner. It was also redolent with years of mustiness and, because I had stayed in rooms like it elsewhere in Asia during my young reportorial years, I could almost see the rats, even though I knew they probably would not come out until after dark." The couple decided to go instead to a new Government Guest House a few blocks away.

Were they to return today, they would be pleasantly surprised. Four years after their visit the Thong Nhat closed for a major face-lift, emerging again in 1992 not only with all its celebrated charm restored but also with its old name. A second phase of development, started in 1994, resulted in a 135-room Opera Wing with a four-story Metropole Centre office tower above it, both of which opened in 1996. Now managed by the Sofitel Group, the Metropole is once more the place to stay in Hanoi for official guests, visiting royalty and such celebrities as Catherine Deneuve and film director Oliver Stone. Fittingly enough, Michael Caine and other cast members stayed there while filming the latest version of *The Quiet American*.

The hotel marked its 100th anniversary in 2001 with a series of events, among them the launches of a cookbook called *La Cusine du Vietnam* by famed chef Didier Corlou and an updated book on its own history, a performance by international musicians at the Opera House across the street and a celebration of films featuring its former guest Charlie Chaplin.

Top: The Metropole has four bars and two restaurants that are renowned for their French and Vietnamese cuisine.

Right: A terrace with swirling roof supports made of iron provide some shade to this girl who is wearing a traditional Vietnamese dress known as an ao-dai.

Top: The main entrance to the Metropole, which is sheltered by an impressive glass canopy. White Grecian-style columns line the building façade along the street.

Bottom: A guest room with a large teakwood bed and a chaise lounge for relaxing. Visitors over the years have ranged from the novelist Graham Greene to the actress Jane Fonda and even Charlie Chaplin.

HOTEL MAJESTIC
HO CHI MINH CITY, VIETNAM
ESTABLISHED 1925

Saigon, as Ho Chi Minh City was known until 1975, was among the world's best-known date-lines during the 50s and early 70s. Journalists came from all over to report (and often to argue about) first, the last days of French colonial rule in Indo-China and then the bitter and ultimately unsuccessful war fought by South Vietnam and the United States against North Vietnam.

Many of these media visitors stayed at the old Continental Hotel on the Rue Catinat (now called Dong Khoi Street), built by the French in 1880, while others adopted the modern Caravelle when it was built in 1956. Some, however, preferred the more elegant, colonial-style Majestic, not far away on the corner of Catinat and Quai de Belgique Streets, overlooking the Saigon River; among them was Graham Greene, one of the first and perhaps the most famous novelist to make literary use of the Vietnamese conflict.

Writing of Greene's time in Vietnam, Tim Curry says "the Majestic Hotel offered opulence much closer to the life Greene enjoyed as a wealthy and famous novelist than to the seedy back-alley rooms inhabited by Tom Fowler, [his] protagonist in *The Quiet American*. Perhaps Greene liked the Majestic because he was somewhat insulated from the dangers of the street. In the cozy central courtyard, lounging around the pool, he could easily have imagined being in Nice or St. Tropez and Greene was a born again Frenchman."

For all its French chic and atmosphere, however, the Majestic was in fact built by the ethnic Chinese Huibon Hoa Company in 1925 as a conscious effort to compete with the Continental, offering 44 rooms on four floors. It managed to survive as such until 1951, when it was acquired by a Frenchman of Corsican origin named Mathieu Franchini, who also owned the Continental and was the son-in-law of a wealthy Vietnamese businessman. In 1965, at the height of the second Vietnam war when Franchini's lease ran out, it came under the management of the National Travel Bureau; two more floors were added in 1968 and the hotel was renamed the Hoan My.

The long period of conflict ended with the re-unification of Vietnam in 1975. Toward the end, Saigon had become, in the words of Jon Swain, "a bloated, booming Sin City... always on the edge of catastrophe; a city of depravity; the Sodom of the East." Returning a decade later, Swain found it "all shabby, rundown, sad. But I felt sure that [it] would rise from the ashes of the war. Down by the river front where, in *The Quiet American*, the fictional Fowler had watched American warplanes being disembarked, there were cargo ships from many nations."

By then the former Majestic, now bearing a new name, the Cuu Long, had a total of 99 guest rooms and both European and Asian restaurants but its former glamour was more than a little tarnished and there were relatively few guests. It remained in this condition for most of the next ten years while both Ho Chi Minh City and the country as a whole struggled to recover. Not until the 1990s did the tourists start coming back and, with them, a demand for hotels that met international standards.

In 1995 the Saigontourist Holding Company was set up to manage several hotels in Vietnam. The Majestic, reverting to its original name, was one of them. It closed for a year, underwent a total renovation costing over five million dollars, and reopened with 122 guestrooms and suites, a business center and a health club.

The mood is still predominantly French, though today it would be a little harder for a visitor to dream of being in Nice or St. Tropez. The roof bar, Tom Curry writes, "has a fine view both up and down the river where you can contemplate the strange flavors of Vietnam from a safe height. Below, sampans share the waterway with high-speed hydrofoils. After dark, above the dark tangle of bamboo scaffolding and corrugated iron shanties on the opposite bank, giant neon billboards advertising Heineken, Phillips and AIWA seem to hang suspended, icons of the reinstated corporate pantheon. Even more incongruous is the mariachi band on the Majestic's open roof deck wearing sombreros and black suits and playing Mexican swing for the tourists." Graham Greene, on the other hand, with his fine sense of irony and his taste for contrasts, might still find the Majestic a congenial place to stay.

Clockwise from top left: Art deco railings line this soaring stairway leading up from the lobby; Intricate architectural details such as this stucco molding may be found throughout the hotel; A statue in classic style stands between towering Grecian columns; The mirrored bar with stained-glass art deco panels above.

Top: The stairway forms an interesting sinuous pattern as it winds through bare white walls.

Page 152: The Majestic in Ho Chi Minh City, formerly known as Saigon. It was built in the mid-1920s, not by the French but by a Chinese-owned company.

Page 153: The opulent lobby of the Majestic. The hotel underwent a number of name changes and owners over the years before it was finally restored to its original splendor in the mid-1990s.

Left: The Majestic's main lobby features tall arched windows and high ceilings; essential design features to ensure that cool air circulated through the building when it was first built.

Clockwise from right: The archways at the hotel entrance display intricate art deco details; Guests have a choice of dining outdoors; The hotel's reception desk incorporates intricate wood carvings; Art deco was very much in vogue when the Hotel Majestic was first built, as this area of the roof garden shows; The hotel's suites are elegantly appointed. Graham Greene stayed at the Majestic when he wrote The Quiet American, *his famous novel set during the Vietnam War.*

SOFITEL DALAT PALACE
DALAT, VIETNAM
ESTABLISHED 1922

Located in Vietnam's central highlands, at an altitude of some 4,900 feet (1,500 meters), Dalat is blessed with cool temperatures that can become downright cold during the winter months. Its earliest inhabitants were Montagnard tribal groups—"Da Lat", in one of the local languages, means "River of the Lat Tribe"—but the town itself was established only in 1912 and quickly became to the French of Saigon and other low-lying areas what the hill-stations of India were to the British: a place where they could escape the heat and relax in a more bracing climate.

A large lake called Xuan Huang (named after a 17th century female poet) was created by the construction of a dam in 1919, adding to the scenic charms of the place. It was soon followed by a summer palace for the Emperor Bao Dai in a pine grove, a Residence for the Governor-General, a Catholic Cathedral in gingerbread style, Buddhist temples with tiered pagodas, a convent built between 1940 and 1942 and over 2,000 European-style villas, mostly owned by colonial French, who often fondly referred to Dalat as Le Petit Paris.

Inevitably, such a popular holiday destination required accommodations for temporary visitors and it got its first luxury hotel, the Langbian Palace, in 1922, owned by the French Administration of Indo-China. Overlooking the lake and featuring spacious rooms with fireplaces to ward off the winter chill, this became the premier place to stay, along with the adjacent Hotel du Parc, which opened in 1932.

Ownership of the hotels changed several times over the years and for a few months in 1945 they were closed, the Langbian Palace being used to accommodate the commander of the occupying Japanese forces. After World War II it again became the property of the French.

However, difficult times came during the French Indo-China war, when getting to Dalat by road from Saigon turned into a dangerous journey, beset by attacks from forces then called the Viet Minh.

In 1950, the writer Norman Lewis had to come in an armed convoy from Saigon, which took thirteen hours through dense jungle and fortified towns. He paused only briefly in the resort before heading further into the highland and was singularly unimpressed. "Dalat is the playground of Indo-China," he wrote in his account of Vietnam called *A Dragon Apparent*, "and has a fair share of the dreariness so often associated with places so advertised." He found it "like a drab little resort in Haute Savoie, developed by someone who has spent a few years as vice-consul in Shanghai."

In 1958 it was given to the South Vietnamese Government and acquired a new name, the Dalat Palace.

Conditions obviously changed when the French left and the war turned into one between South Vietnam, supported by Americans, and the Viet Cong (as the Viet Minh were now known). According to the Lonely Planet guide, during the Vietnam war, "Dalat was, by tacit agreement of all parties, largely spared the ravages of war. Indeed, it seems that while South Vietnamese soldiers were being trained at the city's military academies and affluent officials of the Saigon regime were relaxing in their villas, Viet Cong cadres were doing the same thing not far away in their villas."

Following the final end of fighting, in 1975, management of the Dalat Palace passed to the Lam Dong Tourist Company. In 1991, this company and Danao International Holdings Ltd. formed a joint venture called Dalat Resort Incorporation, which was given the task of renovating the Dalat Palace and the Hotel du Parc, as well as sixteen of the French villas and the emperor's former palace. Work on the Dalat Palace started immediately and on the Hotel du Parc four years later; in 2005 the joint venture became a wholly-owned foreign company, with the villas and the palace returned to the provincial government.

Now called the Hotel Sofitel Dalat Palace, the former Langbian Palace reopened in May of 1995, with 43 elegant guest rooms decorated in colonial style, restaurants specializing in fine French cuisine, and over 2,000 works of art scattered throughout. (The Hotel Du Parc, now the Novotel Dalat, opened in 1997 with 140 rooms.)

Dalat's status as Vietnam's favorite resort has also been restored. Some 300,000 domestic tourists, including many honeymooners, as well as foreign visitors now arrive annually, either by plane (a 35-minute flight from Ho Chin Minh City) or by road (four hours through some of the most beautiful scenery in Asia)

Left: The dining room of Le Rabelais, the hotel's French restaurant, decorated with belle epoque-style paintings. Built in 1922, the Dalat Palace was originally called the Lambian Palace and was a popular hot-season treat for the French who lived in low-lying places like Saigon.

Bottom: Carved wooden railings frame these passageways and look down to the lobby.

Bottom left: Polished hardwood furniture and thick walls kept out the winter chill during the cool months.

Right: Le Rabelais serves French cuisine in an atmosphere of formal elegance; a belle epoque painting is in keeping with the period upholstery used on the chairs.

Page 158: Decorative pieces such as this bronze bust can be found throughout the hotel.

Page 159: Mosquito netting forms graceful bed canopies in one of the hotels 43 guest rooms.

Left: Carefully trimmed hedges and trees create a formal French garden; cool temperatures enable the cultivation of many plants otherwise rarely seen in the tropics.

Bottom: The hotel's wide passageways lend a sense of scale to the belle epoque-style paintings and decor.

Bottom left: The Dalat Palace's restaurant is renowned for serving sumptuous French cuisine and wine.

Right: Larry's Bar gets its name from Larry Hillblom. He was an American businessman who transformed Dalat into a luxurious resort destination. It remains a popular place to enjoy afternoon tea or cocktails.

Bottom right: These steps lead up to the main entrance of the hotel, which is surrounded by a park at the edge of Xuan Huong Lake.

CARCOSA
SERI NEGARA
KUALA LUMPUR, MALAYSIA
ESTABLISHED 1898

Author, explorer and administrator, Frank Swettenham (later Sir Frank) was one of the great figures of British Malaya. In 1896, when Selangor, Negeri Sembilan and Pahang were brought together as the Federated Malay States, he was appointed the federation's first Resident-General. Based in the Selangor capital of Kuala Lumpur, he almost at once set about building a Residency suitable for so eminent a position.

He chose a hilltop site overlooking the beautiful Lake Gardens, which had been laid out in 1888. The name of the architect is uncertain but it was probably A.C. Norman, who also designed St. Mary's Cathedral on the padang in Kuala Lumpur. However, the builders, Mssrs. Nicholas and Walsh are known, and were given 15 months to complete the task, at a cost of more than $67,000 in local currency. The impatient Swettenham moved in before it was finished and had already been receiving guests for several months before the official housewarming party, a costume ball, was held on 28 August 1898.

It was an imposing structure, a large half-timbered, gabled house incorporating several architectural styles and a broad verandah with chocolate-and-cream-colored Minton Hollins tiles especially ordered from Switzerland. The airy entrance hall, rising all the way to the roof, had an ecclesiastical feel and was made of a local hardwood called merbau. From the center, a bifurcated staircase led to a gallery and seven bedrooms; the Resident-General's was the largest, leading onto a spacious verandah above the entrance porch.

Landscaping presented a problem because of the steep hillside—the sloping lawns had to be cut by hand for years—but gradually this was overcome and the range of mature tropical trees and shrubs today add greatly to the Carcosa's appeal. Specimens include a century-old cempaka, a member of the Magnolia family with strongly scented flowers, and *Amherstia nobilis*, which has clusters of coral-colored blossoms and has been described as the most beautiful tree in the tropical world.

Swettenham chose Carcosa as the name of the house for reasons that remained obscure until the 1930s when, in an article, he explained that he had taken it from a book in which there was a castle of the same name. Though Swettenham thought the word was probably coined by the author; it also looked, he wrote: "like a combination of the Italian words *cara* and *cosa* and would mean 'desirable dwelling' as, indeed, I found it."

Two further Resident-Generals lived in the house after Swettenham, after which the post was abolished and replaced by, first, Chief Secretary, and then Federal Secretary. A smaller dwelling just down the hill was added to the grounds in 1913. Originally called the Governor's Residence, later the King's House, and now the Seri Negara ("beautiful house" in Bahasa Malaysia), it was built as a guesthouse for distinguished visitors.

Social functions at Carcosa were very formal in the 1920s and '30s. They ceased when Kuala Lumpur fell to the Japanese on 7 January 1942, after which both buildings were used by senior officers of the Imperial Army. After the war, the property housed a varied collection of people, among them British officers, Ching Ping, leader of the Malayan People's Anti-Japanese Army (who later took up armed struggle in the jungle), and Sir Gerald Templer, who defeated the communists during the long period known as the Emergency.

As independence approached in 1956, Tunku Abdul Rahman, Chief Minister of Malaya, presented the deed to the Carcosa to the British government. A succession of British High Commissioners lived there but political pressure mounted for its return and the British finally handed it over in 1987. Initially it was used as a state guesthouse for foreign dignitaries. Together with the Seri Negara, it later became a first-class hotel, but was made available for government use for a certain number of days each year.

Queen Elizabeth II and Prince Philip (who had already stayed in the Seri Negara on a state visit in 1972) were guests of the Carcosa in 1989, occupying Swettenham's spacious suite of rooms, which had been redecorated in Victorian style. Later it received a long list of other visiting dignitaries.

The Carcosa was renovated again in 1997, acquiring a spa, satellite TV and improved kitchens, while preserving the original appearance of the building. The Seri Negara was renovated in 2001, adding six more suites to the seven in Carcosa.

Guests today find modern conveniences blended with such reminders of the colonial past as Sunday curry tiffins and high tea served on verandahs overlooking the gardens. Only the skyscrapers of downtown Kuala Lumpur, glimpsed through the trees, remind one that a different world exists outside.

Left: The hallway with stairs leading up to the second floor of the Carcosa. It became an official guest house when Malaysia achieved independence in 1956 and was later converted into a boutique hotel.

Top: A dining table on the terrace offers views of the lush tropical gardens that surround the hotel. A ceiling fan above provides air circulation just as it did when the hotel was first built.

Top right: The sitting area of the largest of the hotel's seven spacious suites; the doors open onto a terrace overlooking the garden. A procession of distinguished visitors, including Queen Elizabeth II, have stayed here.

Right: The upper hallway in the Carcosa, with polished hardwood floors and a Persian carpet.

Page 164: A table and wicker chair on the verandah off the main suite, above the entrance driveway.

Page 165: A side view of the Carcosa, built in 1898 on a hilltop site outside Kuala Lumpur as the residence of the first Resident-General of the Federated Malay States.

Top: The hotel offers outdoor dining that allows guests to take in the scenic beauty of the compound. The gardens feature a variety of tropical trees and shrubs, including the Amherstia nobilis, regarded as one of the most beautiful tropical trees in the world.

Bottom: The Carcosa Seri Negara started life as the official home of Frank Swettenham, the first Resident-General of British Malaya. It had seven bedrooms when first built; today this boutique hotel has 13 Victorian-style suites.

Clockwise from right: The entrance to the Carcosa; the large open terrace above the carport is part of the hotel's master suite, while the garden includes a vast variety of ornamental trees and shrubs; Breezy terraces and white columns make the Carcosa a perfect example of residences built for tropical living in the late 19th and early 20th centuries; Wicker furniture with cotton cushions, high ceilings, and louvered windows suggest the past in this corner.

EASTERN
& ORIENTAL HOTEL
PENANG, MALAYSIA
ESTABLISHED 1889

Penang, founded by Captain Francis Light in 1786, was the first British settlement in Malaya. Offering a safe harbor and a strategic position at the northern end of the Straits of Malacca, it prospered as a free port and attracted a highly varied population of Chinese, Malays and Indians, as well as substantial communities of Armenians, Jews, Persians and other races. With the establishment of Singapore, trade and power gradually moved southward but Penang remained an important part of British Malaya, enjoying its most prosperous years in the early 1920s when it was a hub for the rubber plantations and tin mines of the mainland.

Though the Armenian community was never very large—one account estimates that only around 25 lived there in any given year—its influence was considerable. One who arrived around 1882 was Tigran Sarkies, setting up first as an auctioneer and then in 1884, venturing into the hotel business with an establishment called the Eastern Hotel. His brother Martin joined him in the field two years later, opening the Oriental Hotel on a nearby site. Two other Sarkies, Aviet and Arshak, soon became active in the firm called "Sarkies Brothers, Hotel Proprietors," which would eventually spread throughout British colonies in the region.

Tigran moved on to Singapore, where he started the Raffles Hotel in 1887. Meanwhile the two Penang properties were joined to form the much larger Eastern & Oriental Hotel, which opened to enthusiastic reception in 1889. A few years later, Aviet Sarkies, who was said to be the most retiring of the brothers, acquired the Strand Hotel in Rangoon and turned it into an equally grand facility for traveling dignitaries.

After Martin's retirement (he went to Isfahan, Persia, where he married and had three children), the Eastern & Oriental was operated by Arshak, who proceeded to turn it into Penang's leading hotel. A stately white structure with Moorish minarets, a spacious domed lobby and what it boasted was "the longest seafront lawn east of Suez," stretching for 842 feet (255 meters), it soon became popularly known as the E&O. Some asserted the name stood for "Eat and Owe," due to the large number of unpaid chits signed by clients and uncollected by the hospitable Arshak, who was often to be seen dancing around in the ballroom with a glass of whisky and soda balanced on his head. It was a social center for locals and a temporary home for such visiting celebrities as Rudyard Kipling, Douglas Fairbanks, Mary Pickford, Noel Coward, his friend Lord Amherst and (inevitably) Somerset Maugham, who wrote some of his best stories about life in British Malaya there.

Hard times lay ahead, however. Partly because of the collapse of rubber prices in the late 1920s and partly, perhaps, because of Arshak's generosity, business slumped drastically and the hotel went bankrupt in 1931. (Arshak was spared this sad experience; he died a few months before, lauded in the press for his philanthropic spirit and as being "one of the most popular figures in Malaya.") Japanese occupation during World War II was an even more serious blow and though the E&O survived the ordeal it emerged as a mere shadow of its former self.

The hotel changed hands several times in the following years, but few substantial improvements were made. Alexander Frater, a travel writer who came in 1986, found it "humid and shadowy, without the benefit of air-conditioning," though he still admired "the long, trim lawn planted with casuarina and coconut palms," along the sea wall outside his room. While its one-time sister hotels Raffles and the Strand found developers willing to underwrite the expensive task of restoring them—and while similar plans were regularly rumored to be in the works for the E&0—it remained more or less as it was. Its white wedding-cake façade slowly began to peel away, though some travelers continued to stop there out of nostalgia. Its evocative name was even borrowed for a super-luxurious train that runs from Singapore to Bangkok that was started in the mid-90s by the owners of the famed Orient Express.

Renovations at last got underway in 1996, however. The hotel was closed for several years and, after a major restoration and refurbishment program that cost RM75 million, reopened at the dawn of the new millennium. Once more what Arshak Sarkies called "the premier hotel East of Suez," (a slogan, it might be noted, used by his brothers to describe their hotels as well) it once again assumed its central role in Penang's social scene. Complete with sweeping lawn, grand staircase, sea views and, according to the hotel's website, "the oldest Otis lift in Malaysia," its enduring legacy continues.

Left: The lobby of the Eastern and Oriental Hotel or the E&O, as it has long been popularly known, with a dramatic domed ceiling, marble floors and a piano.

Right: Wide, tall doorways that allowed for maximum ventilation were characteristic of hotels built in the late 19th century.

Bottom right: Elegant iron roof supports, classic white columns and potted palms line this outside terrace.

Bottom left: A suite at the hotel contains richly covered colonial-style furniture and an ornate Chinese screen.

Page 170: Pictures of three of the famous Sarkies brothers hang above a table at the E&O. This was the first of several hotels the brothers founded, others being the Raffles in Singapore and the Strand in Yangon.

Page 171: Façade of the Eastern and Oriental. Originally this was two hotels, which were joined together to form a single structure overlooking the seafront in Penang; In 1996 it underwent an extensive renovation to meet the demands of modern travelers, though retaining its classic features.

Clockwise from left: Moorish-style turrets provide an exotic touch to this rooftop terrace, which overlooks coconut palms and the blue waters of the Indian Ocean; An area for sun-bathing on the roof of the hotel; An Agave grows in a classic-style urn overlooking the hotel's swimming pool; Geometric pillars line the hotel's external corridors and provide an interesting visual touch.

Right: The E&O's blue-tiled swimming pool is shaded by slender coconut palms. After years of neglect, the hotel was completely restored and refurnished in the latter part of the 1990s.

Bottom: An attentive staff member stands by to greet guests. The hotel is renowned for its excellent service.

RAFFLES
HOTEL
SINGAPORE
ESTABLISHED 1887

Raffles Hotel, which would become one of the most famous hotels in Asia, began life in 1887 as a humble 10-room bungalow on Singapore's Beach Road, then just a short walk from the bustling port. It was owned by the Armenian Sarkies brothers, and managed by Tigran Sarkies until his death in 1912, when it was taken over by another of the brothers Aviet, more famous for having started the Strand in Rangoon (see page 114).

Tigran Sarkies had lofty ambitions for his hotel from the very start. With the opening of the Suez Canal, an increasing number of ships stopped at Singapore, bringing with them more and more visitors. A pair of two-story wings was added to either side of the bungalow in 1890, as well as a separate billiards room. Soon after, the Palm Court wing was built on an adjacent plot, with an expanse of lawn surrounded by stately palm trees. The old bungalow was replaced in 1899 by a new main building, boasting electric lights, a lofty lobby rising three stories and a dining room that seated 500 guests. The last major addition made by Tigran was the Bras Basah Wing. Opened in 1904, the new wing offered 20 suites on the upper floor and also featured one of Singapore's first shopping centers.

By that time Raffles was already a Singapore landmark. It had its own potent legends and was busily acquiring more. One had it that a man-eating tiger was found and shot under the billiard table in 1904. Actually the animal was an escapee from a circus and had taken refuge under the floor rather than the table, but it was indeed shot (by a teacher from the nearby Raffles Institution) and it was indeed described as "a very hungry specimen" in the local press. More accurate was the story about the fabled Singapore Sling being concocted by a Hainanese bartender named Ngiam Tong Boon in the hotel's Long Bar around 1915.

With the addition of a large ballroom in 1920, the Raffles Hotel became just as popular with locals as it was with visitors. Somerset Maugham, the peripatetic author who stayed in many of Asia's most famous hotels, described it as "standing for all the fables of the exotic east." Charlie Chaplin, Noel Coward and the Prince of Wales were among the famous faces who also came. Rubber planters from British Malaya gathered for lunch in the Tiffin Room and dancing continued in the ballroom, draped with blackout curtains, until only a few weeks before Singapore fell to the Japanese in February 1942.

Though physically unscathed by the war, the Raffles Hotel was unmistakably showing its age by the late 1940s. This increased over the next few decades as Singapore's tourist center gradually shifted to Orchard Road and new hotels offered more amenities than the old structure was able to do. For a time, there was even talk of tearing it down and replacing it with a wholly modern building that was more in keeping with the city's new high-tech image.

Fortunately, though, more sensible heads prevailed. The Raffles Hotel was declared a National Monument in 1987, closed its doors in 1989 and underwent a massive restoration costing some $160 million. 1915 was chosen as the benchmark year, which meant removal of the ballroom and replacing it with an earlier, cast-iron portico. Accuracy was sought down to the smallest detail of decorative plaster work with the help of old photographs and building plans, and period furnishings were collected from various sources. Modern facilities and comforts were also added but in such a way that they blended seamlessly with the atmosphere of the hotel's fabled past.

After two and a half years, what might accurately be described as the new-old Raffles opened on 14 September 1991. It now has 103 spacious suites, including 10 named after such personalities as Somerset Maugham, Noel Coward, Andre Malraux and Ava Gardner (who came for the premiere of one of her films in the 1950s), scattered over five rambling wings linked by broad verandahs overlooking the courtyards. Its tropical gardens contain more than 50,000 plants, ranging from huge bird's nest ferns and fragrant frangipanis to breadfruit trees and traveler's palms with their crown of paddle-shaped leaves.

The towering skyscrapers of new Singapore now rise brashly on reclaimed land that separates Raffles from the seafront by close to a mile. Behind its elegant façade, though, the hotel has succeeded in preserving its nostalgic charm, memorably recalling an almost vanished era.

Left: The famous Long Bar and a pair of Singapore Slings, first concocted by a Raffles bartender around 1915; period lighting figures and leather-covered stools add to the colonial atmosphere.

Top: The Long Bar's decor was inspired by the look of the Malayan plantations of the 1920s. In addition to its signature drink, the Singapore Sling, the bar serves a wide variety of alcoholic and non alcoholic concoctions.

Top right: The Tiffin Room is renowned for its traditional Asian and Indian cuisine and serves a sumptuous lunch and dinner buffet.

Right: A sitting area on the second floor of the hotel's lobby. 1915 was the benchmark year set for the hotel's restoration, and this is reflected in the decor and style of furniture used.

Page 176: Wicker furniture on a terrace outside one of the several courtyards in Raffles.

Page 177: A silver Rolls Royce waits outside the cast-iron portico in front of Raffles. At one time a ballroom stood here but since 1915 was chosen as the benchmark year for the multi-million-dollar restoration of the hotel it was removed to ensure architectural accuracy.

Top left: A table on a terrace on one of the upper verandahs; each suite has such a private space, divided by wooden screens.

Left and top: The grand lobby of the Raffles Hotel has lighting fixtures and furniture in the style of the late-19th century when it originally opened its doors to guests. Great pains were taken during the hotel's restoration to ensure that fittings were as accurate as possible.

Top left: *A guest room furnished with reproductions of antiques to create a soothing atmosphere; the door on the far side opens onto a private sitting area.*

Left: *View from the Palm Court, showing the private areas outside each room.*

Top: *Old-fashioned Chinese-style roof tiles were used throughout in the hotel's restoration, while the towering palms remain from its early days.*

Right: *A room boy walks down one of Raffles' many polished teakwood corridors. Over the years these same corridors have seen the likes of such celebrities as Somerset Maugham, Noel Coward and Charlie Chaplin.*

THE FULLERTON HOTEL
SINGAPORE
ESTABLISHED 1928

When plans were first announced for construction of the Fullerton Building in 1920, the project aroused a certain amount of controversy. To be located at the mouth of the Singapore River, on a site previously occupied by a fort named after Sir Robert Fullerton, Singapore's first governor, it would be the largest building in the city and one of the most costly—a highly visible symbol of what some saw as arrogant extravagance and others as power and prosperity.

The Shanghai-based architectural firm of Keys and Dowdeswell was commissioned to draw up the design, but due to debate about expenses the foundations were not laid until 1924. The building was completed four years later, at a total cost of over four million dollars, regarded as a staggering sum to spend on what was essentially Singapore's main post office.

Sir Hugh Clifford, then Governor, presided over the opening on 26 June 1928. Reporting the event the following day, the *Straits Times* commented, "The Post Office Building, with its walls towering 120 feet from the ground, its fluted Doric colonnades on their heavy base, its lofty portico over the main entrance and the 400-foot frontage along the waterfront, adds immeasurably to both the dignity and solidity of central Singapore… The general verdict is that the architects have made the most of a great opportunity and that all who have had a share in the building have enhanced their professional reputation."

The impressive building, overlooking Fullerton Square in the heart of the city, linked the harbor, the government office of Empress Place, and the commercial center of Raffles Place. It became one of Singapore's most prominent landmarks, appearing on numerous postcards in the 1930s. The post office occupied the basement and two floors as sorting rooms, postal halls, and offices, while an area along Collyer Quay was used to transfer mail to waiting ships. At other times in its early history, the Fullerton also housed the Chamber of Commerce, the exclusive Singapore Club and the Inland Revenue Authority. A lighthouse atop the building guided ships approaching the busy harbor.

Its stout walls made it a haven when the Japanese attacked with bombs and shells in 1942 and the lower floor was turned into a makeshift hospital filled with wounded soldiers and civilians. On 13 February 1942, known as Black Friday, the end was obviously near. That day, Sir Shenton Thomas, the Commander-in-Chief of the Straits Settlement and High Commissioner of the Malay States, and his wife abandoned Government House, which had been repeatedly shelled, and took refuge in the Singapore Club along with several hundred other VIPS.

They were there when Singapore surrendered two days later, and on 17 February, dressed in a newly pressed white duck suit, Sir Shenton crossed nearby Anderson Bridge and joined the long procession of men, women and children forced to walk under the hot sun on their way to internment in Changi Prison.

After the war, the Fullerton resumed its role as the central post office as well as housing several government offices. The square outside was the scene of many election campaign rallies that marked the end of British rule and the emergence of Singapore as an independent state. For all its stately beauty, however, the massive building increasingly became an anachronism as the city expanded in other directions and as such offices as the Board of Trade and the Ministry of Finance moved into more modern quarters; the lighthouse ceased operations in 1978 and the post office moved in 1996.

As the new millennium approached, however, a new role was found for the Fullerton. It was acquired by the Sino Land Company, one of the largest property developers in Hong Kong, and the Far East Organization, an affiliate in Singapore, and work began on transforming it into a grand hotel. The effort, which took three years and cost some S$400 million, required both dedication and determination. As a historic building the Fullerton was treated with respect, its façade carefully preserved while a modern, high-tech hotel was created inside. The Doric columns, coffered ceilings, cornices and Italian marble floors were restored to their original splendor; in some cases, exceptionally fine interior work was revealed after being hidden by earlier renovations for many years.

The new hotel has 400 rooms and suites, either overlooking the sunlit atrium courtyard or with balconies offering

Top: A lofty airiness characterizes the hotel's lobby (left), which combines many of its old features with highly modern additions (right).

Left: A stair in the hotel, with a huge glazed jar in keeping with the building's impressive proportions.

Right: The lobby of the Fullerton, with towering columns and Italian marble floors. The Singapore post office once occupied this floor as well as the floor above and the basement. Guest rooms have been created on the upper levels.

Page 184: Modern entrance to the restored Fullerton, which opened on New Year's Day in 2001.

Page 185: Overlooking Singapore's teeming harbor, the Fullerton was the largest building in the city when it was constructed in 1928. It served as the main post office and headquarters of the exclusive Singapore Club.

panoramic views of Singapore's skyline, the promenade along the river, or Marina Bay. The lighthouse on top was also preserved and now serves as an intimate restaurant.

The Fullerton Hotel held its grand opening on New Year's Day 2001, and in July of that year received the Urban Redevelopment Authority Architectural Heritage Award, Singapore's highest honor for contributions towards the protection and restoration of the city's built heritage. In 2002, it appeared on *Condé Nast Traveller* magazine's list of the world's top new hotels.

Clockwise from far left: Contemporary pieces such as this stainless steel sidetable added a modern touch to the Fullerton's neo-classical architecture; Located in the heart of Singapore's Central Business District, the Fullerton's rooms are designed to provide business travelers with luxurious accomodations; The Fullerton's use of color and open public spaces emphasize the building's clean lines; The hotel's two-story Loft Suites offer spectacular views of Singapore's waterfront.

Right: Rear view of the Fullerton with its Doric columns and a modern swimming pool and views of downtown Singapore.

Bottom: With the Singapore River in the foreground, the floodlit Fullerton is one of the most imposing colonial buildings in the city. A lighthouse on the roof once signaled ships in the harbor behind.

SAVOY HOMANN
BANDUNG, INDONESIA
ESTABLISHED 1939

In 1884 a railway line was completed between the Dutch colonial capital of Batavia (now Jakarta) to the relatively small and isolated city of Bandung on a high plateau surrounded by volcanic peaks. With that achievement, a mere two and a half hour train ride was all it took to leave behind sweltering, malarial Batavia and luxuriate in the cool highlands, where temperatures rarely rose above 75 degrees Fahrenheit (24 degrees Celsius) and shady trees lined the streets.

Already chichona (quinine) trees from South America, tea from Assam and coffee from Brazil had been introduced to the area and Bandung enjoyed a considerable degree of prosperity. (There was also a darker side to this agricultural activity: it was responsible for the notorious Forced Cultivation System, under which countless Javanese worked on the plantations as virtual slave labor for some 200 years of Dutch rule.) With the new railway, however, growth accelerated, bringing new hotels, shops, restaurants and other facilities for planters who came down from their homes in the highlands and visitors who arrived from the capital in search of rest and recreation; the Concordia Society opened a club house with a large ballroom that became the center of local social life. Bandung was proudly called the "Paris of the East" and the comparison may have seemed apt during its heyday in the 1920s and 30s.

The Savoy Homann soon became the preferred place to stay. The original hotel on the site, a one-story neo-classical structure with open verandahs, was erected toward the end of the 19th century and according to some stories, a grand party was held there to celebrate the arrival of the railway. (It is not known when the Homanns came to Indonesia, but they were Germans, not, as often suggested, Dutch.) In 1939 it was almost completely rebuilt by a noted architect named A.F. Aalbers, who came to Bandung in 1930 and whose firm, Aalbers van den Waal, had already designed several homes and office buildings, among them the Denis Insurance Company (now the Bank of West Java) which is similar to the Savoy Homann though not as striking.

The new structure was in art deco style, with elegant horizontal lines formed by the room corridors with porthole-like windows adorning the façade, an imposing tower that made a strong vertical statement, an inner garden and one of the first elevators ever seen in Bandung. Some parts of the older hotel also remained, such as a wing with deco stained-glass windows that probably dated from the 1920s and a separate two-story wing built around 1915 to house the staff. The last was reportedly used during the war by the Japanese secret police, while the hotel itself was reserved for Japanese officers.

An imposing list of famous people have stayed at the Savoy Homann, some even before it assumed its present form, among them the Governor-General of French Indochina, the Duchess of Westminster and the King and Queen of Siam. On his second trip to Indonesia in 1936, Charlie Chaplin was a guest together with the actress Paulette Goddard. (Chaplin had stayed at another hotel in Bandung, the Preanger, when he came in 1931 and later wrote that it was the only place in that part of Java where he could have a real European-style bath.) In more modern times, the hotel has welcomed such national leaders as President Pandit Jawaharal Nehru of India, Foreign Minister Chou En Lai of China and President Gamal Abdul Nasser of Egypt. They were there in 1955 to attend the Afro-Asian Conference to launch the non-aligned movement, organized by Indonesia's President Sukarno (who, incidentally, received his engineering diploma in 1926 from the famous Bandung Institute of Technology).

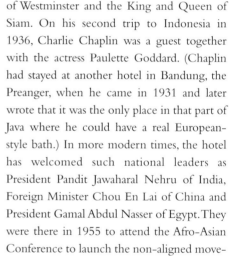

When the Savoy Homann was acquired by a company called PT Panghegar in 1989, the complex consisted of five buildings: the original three from pre-war days, one added in 1955 to accommodate guests attending the Conference and one erected in 1986. The new owners immediately embarked on a program of loving restoration and conservation, of which a large part consisted of eliminating nearly all of the decorations—Javanese woodcarvings, cement statues and wall murals—that had been added over the years.

Visits to other Aalbers-designed buildings in the city persuaded them that the architect favored unadorned sculptural effects, suggested by the way he curved walls in stairwells so that one could stand strategically and see repeated waves of receding cornices and moldings. Lowered ceilings of teak and black paneling were removed, thus restoring rooms to their original

Top: A guest room; art deco styles were retained in the hotel when it was restored in the early 1990s.

Bottom: White walls with muted wooden panels create a mood of elegant simplicity, as in this corridor. During the restoration, as much of the architect's distinctive style was retained as possible.

Clockwise from left: Architect A.F. Aalbers' preference for unadorned scultural effects can be seen in the clean lines of this passageway; Art deco style is evident in this lamp and the detail work on the pillar; Great pains were taken to preserve the hotel's art deco style during its extensive restoration.

Page 190: Entrance to the Savoy Homann; the first hotel on this site was built toward the end of the 19th century and then completely rebuilt in 1930.

Page 191: The sweeping lines of the Savoy Homann, designed by A.F. Aalbers, a noted architect who was responsible for a number of other buildings and houses in Bandung, which served as the summer capital during Dutch colonial days.

elevations. Everything was painted white and marble staircases were stripped of their carpet covering. When it became necessary to have a lower ceiling in the ballroom, it was hung carefully so as to preserve a higher one beautifully decorated with molded scallops that had been revealed during construction work. A swimming pool was added to the property and—with some regret, as it was not part of Aalber's original design—a glass front door to keep out traffic noises and pollution from the street outside.

The hotel is currently operated by Bidakara, the hotel group of Bank Indonesia and, the Savoy Homman's majority shareholder. PT Panghegar still own 20% of the shares in the hotel, which remains one of the most unique architectural designs in Bandung.

Left: The Savoy Homann's clean lines and curving balconies are typical of the hotel's art deco style and give it one of the most stunning façades in Bandung.

Right: The chandeliers, curved skylights and design details on the pillars effectively highlight the hotel's art deco design.

Bottom right: Curving room balconies, seen here from the garden Atrium Coffee Shop, are also used inside the Savoy Homann. These and the art deco columns help give the hotel its unique lines.

Bottom: The entrance to the swimming pool, which was added during the restoration.

MANDARIN ORIENTAL
HOTEL MAJAPAHIT
SURABAYA, INDONESIA
ESTABLISHED 1910

Located in the heart of Surabaya, Indonesia's second largest city and a fabled trading port since the 15th century, the Majapahit has gone by a variety of names over its long history. The hotel was called the Oranje when it first threw open its doors in 1910. It was built by Lucas Martin Sarkies of the famous Armenian family whose collection of grand hotels included the Raffles in Singapore, the Strand in Rangoon and the Eastern and Oriental in Penang.

As a major port, even busier than the capital of Batavia (Jakarta), Surabaya attracted a considerable number of traders and Dutch officials, for whom the elegant Oranje became the preferred place to stay. Within a few decades these were joined by a small but select group of adventurous world travelers en route to the island of Bali, a short ferry ride away and just beginning to acquire its magical reputation. Charlie Chaplin and Paulette Goddard, who may or may not have been his wife at the time (there is some dispute on the matter), were on such a journey in 1936 and attended the opening of a new addition to the front of the hotel, built in the then-fashionable art deco style. Besides forming the lobby, it also contained a cake and ice cream shop, as well as another selling stationery.

World War II, which reached Java in 1942, brought a different kind of guest. Taken over by the Japanese, the Oranje served first as a military barracks, then as a temporary prison for Dutch women and children before they were moved to far less salubrious camps elsewhere and finally as a hotel called the Yamato. In a way though, the most eventful moment in the hotel's history came in September 1945 when British troops landed in Surabaya, a month after the war ended. Their ostensible purpose was to disarm the Japanese, release Allied prisoners-of-war, and serve as caretakers until the Dutch could take over again. They found themselves, however, in the middle of another war that had already begun with the proclamation of Indonesian independence that same month in Jakarta by Nationalists who were determined to end Dutch rule as well as Japanese occupation.

Early on the morning of 19 September 1945, a pro-colonial group raised the red, white, and blue Dutch flag on the hotel's main flagpole. A crowd of angry Indonesians who had gathered in front promptly raised a cry of "Merdeka!" (freedom), lowered the offending flag, and tore off the bottom blue strip,

thus turning it into the Indonesian flag. Confusion and tragedy ensued. A British commander was murdered in October and a full-scale invasion was launched the following month, beginning on 10 November 1945.

During what is known as the Battle of Surabaya, which involved fierce fighting between British forces and poorly armed Indonesian "rebels", the Oranje was briefly known as the Hotel Merdeka. The Nationalists were driven out of the city and into the nearby hills, but to the world they had demonstrated their determination and the days of Dutch rule were clearly numbered. Freedom was finally achieved in December 1949, though not without further struggle and a good deal of pressure from the United Nations. 10 November is celebrated nationally as Heroes Day and Surabaya is called "The City of Heroes" with an appropriate monument to mark the famous battle.

For a time beginning in 1946 the hotel was once more managed by the Sarkies family and underwent yet another name change, being called the Hotel L.M.S. (after its founder Lucas Martin Sarkies). It continued as such until 1969 when a new group of owners decided to call it the Majapahit, after one of ancient Indonesia's most enduring kingdoms. This name, its fifth in nearly 60 years, was retained in 1993 when the property was purchased by the Indonesian Sekar Group and also three months later when a management agreement was signed with the prestigious Mandarin Oriental Hotel Group. There followed a two-year restoration costing some $35 million, after which the Majapahit reopened to claim once more its position as Suyabaya's premier hotel.

Today, the hotel offers 150 luxurious guest rooms and suites, 20 Majapahit Club Rooms featuring exclusive butler service, gold-plated bathroom fixtures and other amenities, a spa, health club and business center. For guests interested in exploring Surabaya and other attractions in East Java, it organ-

izes personalized visits to 100 selected destinations, ranging from local markets and boat rides along the Brantas River through the heart of the city to volcanoes and hill towns in the countryside.

A special treat, started on the hotel's 92nd anniversary, is a daily Duck Parade held at teatime in the art deco lobby. 14 ducks, specially trained by the concierge staff, march along a red carpet through the lobby and out into the manicured lawn of the South Garden. Here they splash around in a fountain pool before retiring to their own private quarters on the hotel grounds. A former manager explained the unusual performance as follows: "The informality of parading ducks through a lobby built in 1936, then allowing them to frolic in the South Garden's fountain is in keeping with our hospitality attitude and style. We encourage the staff to be spontaneous, warm and friendly with each other and their guests, while preserving a dignified sense of service with history."

Clockwise from far left: Stunning art deco details, such as this stained-glass window and lamp can be found through-out the hotel; The hotel's passageways have seen guests from all walks of life over the years, from Dutch colonialists, to Japanese soldiers and Indonesian nationalists; Intricate wrought iron gates open into the hotel's garden; Period furniture and art deco stained glass panels help recreate the hotel's original atmosphere.

Right: The Hotel Majapahit's main restaurant serves various European and Asian favorites, including seafood specialties.

Bottom: The garden at the rear of the Hotel Majapahit is planted with a variety of tropical trees and shrubs. In 1946, the hotel was at the center of a fierce battle between pro and anti-colonial groups, leading Surabaya to be celebrated as "The City of Heroes."

THE TJAMPUHAN HOTEL
BALI, INDONESIA
ESTABLISHED 1928

"I went there half-unwillingly," Geoffrey Gorer wrote of his visit to the island of Bali in the 1930s, "for I expected an uninteresting piece of ballyhoo, picturesque and faked to a Hollywood standard; I left convinced that I had seen the nearest approach to Utopia that I am ever likely to see."

Most of the other Westerners who came to Bali in the 1920s and '30s shared this sense of having discovered an earthly paradise and a number of them, such as the Mexican-born artist Miguel Covarrubias, ended up staying there for prolonged periods of time, using Bali as both subject and inspiration for photography, fiction, painting, dance and anthropological studies. Few Westerners however, left a more lasting impression on Balinese arts and culture than a young German aristocrat named Walter Spies.

The son of a diplomat and born in 1895, Spies had lived in Czarist Russia, Germany and Holland before an urge to experience life in the Far East led him to travel to Java when he was just 28 years old. The young traveler lived for several years in the palace of the Sultan of Yogyakarta, where he conducted an orchestra and began the first of his haunting, stylized paintings. A visit to Bali in 1925 so impressed him that he moved there two years later. Spies decided to setttle not beside the sea like most of the other Europeans, but up in the hills at Ubud instead, which he set about transforming into a center of Balinese art.

After staying for a while in the palace of the ruling family, he began building a collection of thatched-roof bamboo bungalows for himself down one side of a ravine at a place called Campuan, meaning "Where Two Rivers Meet." Here he began a legendary lifestyle that lasted just over a decade and that made him Bali's most famous host as well as a profound influence on almost every aspect of its culture.

Besides his paintings (which now fetch enormous prices whenever one turns up for sale), Spies was involved with woodcarving (encouraging artisans to make their works more realistic), with dance (together with Katharane Mershon he more or less invented the spectacular, all-male Kecak Dance) and with music (he had his own gamelan orchestra for regular performances). Almost every notable visitor came to his two-story bungalow at Campuan, often staying in one of its several outbuildings and enjoying the many pleasures it offered, among them a swimming pool, lavish nightly entertainments and above all, Spies' enormous personal charm and gracious hospitality. Noel Coward, who spent three weeks there in 1934, described the house as being "on the edge of, almost in, the jungle, with monkeys and cranes in the garden and indoors two Steinways and a python"; he was angry to discover Spies had none of his extraordinary paintings for sale, and furious when he discovered later that Charles Chaplin and Barbara Hutton, two earlier guests, had managed to acquire several.

The latter part of Spies life was tragic. Arrested on a morals charge by the puritanical Dutch in 1938, he was imprisoned for a period of eight months (during which his orchestra came to play outside the prison). Then, when Germany invaded Holland at the start of World War II, he was interned as an enemy alien. Two years later, while he was being transferred by sea to Ceylon, a Japanese submarine sank the ship carrying Spies and other internees and he tragically drowned.

His famous house remained, however, and when a new generation of tourists rediscovered Bali's magic in the 1960s (Thai Airways started the first jet service there in 1967), it became the centerpiece of a luxury boutique hotel called the Tjampuhan. Today the hotel has a swimming pool fed by natural spring water, a spa and over 50 Balinese-style bungalow rooms. The complex spills down a hillside overlooking the River Oos, just outside Ubud and has the same jungle-like luxuriance it did during Spies' day, with shrines, statuary, ponds and the soothing sound of water trickling through streams everywhere.

One almost expects a slim, impeccably dressed German to appear at any moment, suggesting an evening of unforgettable dance and music in a setting of unsurpassed beauty—"the last paradise," as one of those early visitors described it.

Left: An open, breezy room looking out to the garden; the panels are carved by local craftsmen and the lamp is in colonial style.

Bottom left: The swimming pool of the Tjampuhan, fed by water from a natural spring on the property; a traditional Balinese figure stands on the left, carved by one of the many artisans who make Ubud a center of local crafts.

Top: Balinese homes tend to be open, like this sitting area almost engulfed by tropical foliage.

Bottom: As can be seen from this view, the Tjampuhan consists of a number of structures at different levels down a steep ravine in Ubud; panoramic vistas are characteristic of the Walter Spies house.

Page 202: Scarlet hibiscus flowers serve as offerings to many of the statues and shrines in Balinese gardens.

Page 203: Part of the Tjampuhan, built in the late 1920s as a residence for Walter Spies. He was a painter who not only had an enduring influence on Balinese art but also entertained most of the island's noted pre-war visitors.

HOTEL LIST

The Peninsula Hotel
Salisbury Road, Kowloon, Hong Kong, SAR
Tel: +852 2920 2888 Fax: +852 2722 4170
E-mail: phk@peninsula.com
www.hongkong.peninsula.com

The Imperial
Janpath, New Delhi 110001, India
Tel: +91 11 2334 1234 Fax: +91 11 2334 2255
E-mail: luxury@theimperialindia.com
www.theimperialindia.com

The Taj Mahal Palace & Tower
Apollo Bunder, Mumbai 400 001, India
Tel: + 91 22 6665 3366 Fax: +91 22 6665 0323
E-mail: tmhresv.bom@tajhotels.com
www.tajhotels.com

The Oberoi Cecil
Chaura Maidan, Shimla,
Himachal Pradesh 171 001, India
Tel: +91 177 280 4848 Fax: +91 177 281 1024
E-mail: gm@oberoi-cecil.com
www.oberoicecil.com

Shiv Niwas Palace
The City Palace, Udaipur 313001
Rajasthan, India
Tel: +91 294 252 8016 Fax: +91 294 252 8006
E-mail:crs@udaipur.hrhindia.com
www.hrhhotels.com

Taj Lake Palace
Lake Pichola, Udaipur 313 001
Rajasthan, India
Tel: +91 294 2528 800 Fax: +91 294 252 8700
E-mail: lakepalace.udaipur@tajhotels.com
www.tajhotels.com

Dwarika's Hotel
Battisputali, Kathmandu, Nepal
Tel: +977 1 447 3725 Fax: +977 1 447 1379
E-mail: info@dwarikas.com
www.dwarikas.com

Ananda in the Himalayas
The Palace Estate, Narendra Nagar
Tehri-Garhwal, Uttaranchal 249175, India
Tel: +91 1378 227 500 Fax: +91 1378 227 550
E-mail: sales@anandaspa.com
www.anandaspa.com

Galle Face Hotel
Galle Road, Colombo 3, Sri Lanka
Tel: +94 11 254 1010 Fax: +94 11 254 1072
E-mail: reservations@gallefacehotel.net
www.gallefacehotel.com

Mount Lavinia Hotel
100 Hotel Road, Mount Lavinia, Sri Lanka
Tel: +94 11 271 5221 7 Fax: +94 11 273 0726
E-mail: mount.lavinia@mtlavinia.com
www.mountlaviniahotel.com

Amangalla
Church Street, Fort Galle, Sri Lanka
Tel: +94 91 223 3388 Fax: +94 91 223 3355
E-mail: amangalla@amanresorts.com
www.amanresorts.com

Taprobane Island
Weligama, Sri Lanka
Tel: +94 91 438 0275 Fax: +94 91 222 2624
E-mail: sunhouse@sri.lanka.net
www.taprobaneisland.com

Grand Hotel
Nuwara Eliya, Sri Lanka
Tel: +94 52 222 2881 Fax: +94 52 222 2264
E-mail: grand@sltnet.lk
www.tangerinehotels.com

The Strand
92 Strand Road, Yangon, Myanmar
Tel: +95 1 243 377 Fax: +95 1 243 393
E-mail: strand@ghmhotels.com
www.ghmhotels.com

The Oriental, Bangkok
48 Oriental Avenue, Bangkok, Thailand 10500
Tel: +66 2 659 9000 Fax: +66 2 659 0000
E-mail: orbkk-enquiry@mohg.com
www.mandarinoriental.com

Sofitel Central Hua Hin Resort
1 Damnernkasem Road
77110 Hua Hin Thailand
Tel: +66 32 512 021 Fax: +66 32 511 014
E-mail: reservation@sofitel.co.th
www.sofitel.com

Raffles Grand Hotel d'Angkor
1 Vithei Charles de Gaulle
Khum Svay Dang Kum
Siem Reap, Kingdom of Cambodia
Tel: +855 63 963 888 Fax: +855 63 963 168
E-mail: siemreap@raffles.com
www.siemreap.raffles.com

Raffles Hotel Le Royal
92 Rukhak Vithei Daun Penh
Off Monivong Boulevard, Sangkat Wat Phnom
Phnom Penh, Kingdom of Cambodia
Tel: +855 23 981 888 Fax: +855 23 981 168
E-mail: phnompenh@raffles.com
www.phnompenh.raffles.com

Sofitel Metropole Hanoi
15 Ngo Quyen Street, 10,000 Hanoi, Vietnam
Tel: +84 4 826 6919 Fax: +84 4 826 6920
E-mail: sofitelhanoi@hn.vnn.vn
www.sofitel.com

Hotel Majestic
1 Dong Khoi Street, District 1
Ho Chi Minh City, Vietnam
Tel: +84 8 829 5517 Fax: +84 8 829 5510
E-mail: sales@majesticsaigon.com.vn
www.majesticsaigon.com.vn

Sofitel Dalat Palace
2 Tran Phu Street, 0 Dalat, Vietnam
Tel: +84 63 825 444 Fax: +84 63 825 457
E-mail: sofitel@vnn.vn
www.sofitel.com

Carcosa Seri Negara
Taman Tasik Perdana
50480 Kuala Lumpur, Malaysia
Tel: +603 2295 0888 Fax: +603 2282 7888
E-mail: carcosa@ghmhotels.com
www.carcosa.com.my

Eastern and Oriental Hotel
10 Lebuh Farquhar, 10200 Penang, Malaysia
Tel: +604 222 2000 Fax: +604 261 6333
E-mail: reservations@e-o-hotel.com
www.e-o-hotel.com

Raffles Hotel
1 Beach Road, Singapore 189673
Tel: +65 6337 1886 Fax: +65 6339 7650
E-mail: singapore-raffles@raffles.com
www.singapore-raffles.raffles.com

The Fullerton Hotel
1 Fullerton Square, Singapore 049178
Tel: +65 6733 8388 Fax: +65 6735 8388
E-mail: info@fullertonhotel.com
www.fullertonhotel.com

Savoy Homann Bidakara Hotel
Jalan Asia Afrika No. 112, Bandung 40261
West Java, Indonesia
Tel: +62 22 423 2244 Fax: +62 22 423 6187
E-mail: savoy@bdg.centrin.net.id
www.savoyhomann-hotel.com

Hotel Majapahit, Mandarin Oriental
65 Jalan Tunjungan, Surabaya 60275
East Java, Indonesia
Tel: +62 31 545 4333 Fax: +62 31 545 4111
E-mail: mandarin@rad.net.id
www.mandarinoriental.com

Tjampuhan Hotel
Jalan Raya Campuhan, Ubud 80571
Gianyar, Bali, Indonesia
Tel: +62 21 975 368 Fax: +62 21 975 137
E-mail: tjampuhan@indo.net.id
www.tjampuhan.com

ACKNOWLEDGEMENTS

The author would like to express his gratitude to Faa Praharnpap for her skillful and imaginative use of internet facilities and thus providing many historical details that would have otherwise been overlooked.

The photographer would like to thank many people for their help and generosity. Without them, we could never have published this book:

In particular a big thank you to Chami Jotisalikorn for her assistance and great company in Sri Lanka and South Vietnam. The generous but demanding task master, Aruna Dhir at the Imperial; Tom Racette who kindly facilitated with all the Sofitel hotels; the enigmatic Geoffrey Dobbs and Henri Tatham from Taprobane and the Sun Hotel Group; Chairman Sanjiv Gardiner and Josephine from Colombo's glorious Galle Face Hotel; and a very big thank you to the General Manager of the Grand Hotel in Sri Lanka. Colin Hall at Ananda in the Himalayas; Sabina Bailey and General Manager Mr Subramanian at Shiv Newas Palace; the inimitable Olivia Richli at Amangalla and Trina Dingle-Ebert of Aman Resorts. Elizabeth Dass from the Eastern & Oriental Hotel in Penang; the lovely staff at the Strand in Rangoon; Lamey Chang from Hong Kong's Peninsula Hotel and Somsri (Susie) Hansirisawasdi from the Oriental in Bangkok. Ms Nguyen Thanh Thuy at the Metropole in Hanoi and the staff at the Metropole; Martijn Van Der Valk from Carcosa Sri Negara and the GHM management in Singapore; Annie Choy from Raffles Hotel Group; Dennis Wong from The Hotel Royal Phnom Penh and the Grand Hotel D'Angkor; Joy Koh and Susie Lim-Kannan of the Fullerton Hotel; Rukman de Fonseka in Colombo, Debbie Fordyce, Mari Morimoto and Julian Davidson for their continuing support and friends everywhere.

Page 206: The Hotel Majapahit was named Hotel Oranje when it first opened in 1910 during the days of Dutch colonial rule.

Bottom: The imposing façade of the Taj Mahal, with its distinctive domes. It has become one of India's most famous landmarks, featuring a blend of fanciful architectural styles.

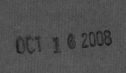

OCT 1 6 2008

SIEM-RÉAP

RANGOON. STRAND HOTEL BURMA.